WRITERS AND THEIR W

ISOBEL ARMSTRONG
General Editor

KAZUO ISHIGURO

KAZUO ISHIGURO

KAZUO ISHIGURO

CYNTHIA F. WONG

Northcote House
in association with the
British Council

First published in 2000 by Northcote House Publishers Ltd, Horndon, Tavistock, Devon, PL19 9NQ, United Kingdom.
Tel: +44 (01822) 810066 Fax: +44 (01822) 810034.

British Library Cataloguing in Publication Data
A catalogue record for this book is available from the British Library

ISBN 0-7463-0861-2

Typeset by PDQ Typesetting, Newcastle-under-Lyme
Printed and bound in Great Britain by
The Baskerville Press, Salisbury, Wiltshire, SP1 3UA

Contents

Acknowledgements

The author gratefully acknowledges The Putnam Publishing Group for permission to quote from *A Pale View of Hills* and *An Artist of the Floating World*; and Faber & Faber and Random House for permission to quote from *The Remains of the Day* and *The Unconsoled*.

Many thanks to the University of Colorado at Denver and the Department of English for faculty research grants and a course release to assist the completion of this book; to Thomas M. Long for his research assistance; to Howard Mills for his perceptive reading of the typescript; to Brian Hulme and Professor Isobel Armstrong for their editorial guidance; and to Kazuo Ishiguro for his gracious and illuminating replies to written and verbal queries about his life and work.

This book is dedicated to Vance A. Crummett and to our daughter, Grace A. Crummett.

Biographical Outline

1954	Kazuo Ishiguro born 8 November to Shizuo and Shizuko Ishiguro in Nagasaki, Japan.
1960	Ishiguro family (including Kazuo's older sister Fumiko; sister Yoko born in Britain) moves to Guildford, Surrey.
1960–6	Attends Stoughton Primary School.
1966–73	Attends World King County Grammar School.
1973–4	Completes schooling. Grouse-beater for the Queen Mother at Balmoral Castle. Employed at Cow & Gate firm packing baby products and inspecting quality of childbirthing films.
1974	Travels to American west coast and British Columbia with backpack. First attempts at writing fiction recorded in travel diary. Completes but does not publish autobiographical fiction. Begins first year at University of Kent at Canterbury in October with studies in English and Philosophy.
1975	Takes a year out after first part of university education. Begins 'dabbling seriously' in fiction.
1976	Community worker at housing estate in Scotland. First view of life away from middle-class upbringing. Exposed to politics of Glasgow through trade-union movement.
1978	Graduates from the University of Kent at Canterbury.
1979	Works with homeless in London and lives in a hostel. Meets Lorna MacDougal. Attends University of East Anglia in October to study Creative Writing. Meets Angela Carter, who becomes his mentor. Meets Malcolm Bradbury and Paul Bailey. Writing career 'begins'.

1980	First story, 'Bananas', published. Graduates from University of East Anglia. Moves to Cardiff, Wales.
1981	Meets editorial director Robert McCrum at Faber, who publishes three of Ishiguro's short stories in *Introductions 7: Stories by New Writers*. Goes to London under McCrum and is commissioned to write *A Pale View of Hills*, which is completed in April. Signs on with literary agents Deborah Rogers and Amanda Urbans. Short story, 'Family Supper', published by *uarto* under Craig Green. Moves to London with Lorna MacDougal.
1982	Continues social work for Cyrenians, especially with housing for the homeless. *A Pale View of Hills* is published and wins the Winifred Holtby Prize of the Royal Society of Literature. The first novel is commissioned for translation in thirteen languages. Commissioned by Channel 4 to write two television dramas, *A Profile of Arthur J. Mason* (transmitted October 1984), and *The Gourmet* (transmitted January 1987). Begins career as a full-time writer.
1983	Listed 'Best of Young British Writers' by the Book Marketing Council.
1986	Publishes *An Artist of the Floating World*, which is shortlisted for the Booker Prize and wins the Whitbread Book of the Year Award. On best-sellers' list in Great Britain and America. His novels translated in over a dozen languages. Begins extensive travels throughout the world. Marries Lorna MacDougal.
1989	Publishes *The Remains of the Day*, which wins the Booker Prize in October. Sonny Mehta becomes his editor at Knopf in America and solidifies Ishiguro's reputation in the States. Goes to Japan for first time in over thirty years under the auspices of Japan Foundation Short-Term Visitors Programme.
1991	Angela Carter dies. Harold Pinter begins screenplay for *The Remains of the Day*.
1992	Meets with Merchant–Ivory Productions to work on big-screen film of *The Remains of the Day*. Daughter, Naomi, born in March.
1993	Merchant–Ivory Productions put out *The Remains of the Day*, which earns eight Oscar nominations. Listed by Granta among Best British Writers.

1994   Serves as jury member at Cannes Film Festival and spends a fortnight in the close company of childhood hero Clint Eastwood and other jurors (Quentin Tarantino's *Pulp Fiction* is the winner that year).

1995   Publishes *The Unconsoled* to mixed reviews. Works on original screenplay with James Ivory. Decorated by the Queen with the OBE for service to literature. Awarded the Premio Scano for literature in Italy. *The Unconsoled* is awarded the Cheltenham Prize at the literary festival. Robert McCrum leaves publishing. Japanese film-maker Kiju Yoshida prepares filming of *A Pale View of Hills* in Japan and Canada.

1998   Awarded the Chevalier dans l'Ordre des Arts et Lettres in France for contribution to literature and culture. Continues work on next novel.

2000   Publishes *When We Were Orphans* with Faber & Faber in London.

Abbreviations and References

AFW   *An Artist of the Floating World* (New York: Vintage International, 1989)

CW   Cynthia Wong, conversation with Kazuo Ishiguro, 3 Sept. 1998

CW2   Cynthia Wong, conversation with Kazuo Ishiguro, 29 Sept. 1999

DOK   Dylan Otto Krider, 'Rooted in a Small Space: An Interview with Kazuo Ishiguro', *Kenyan Review*, 20/2 (1998), 146–54

GM   Gregory Mason, 'An Interview with Kazuo Ishiguro', *Contemporary Literature*, 30/3 (1989), 335–47

KO   Kenzaburo Oe and Kazuo Ishiguro, 'The Novelist in Today's World: A Conversation', *Boundary 2*, 18/3 (1991), 109–22

MJ   Maya Jaggi, 'Kazuo Ishiguro Talks to Maya Jaggi', *Wasafiri*, 22 (1995), 20–4

PVH   *A Pale View of Hills* (New York: Vintage International, 1990)

RD   *The Remains of the Day* (New York: Vintage International, 1993)

SS   Sybil Steinberg, *Publisher's Weekly*, 18 Sept. 1995, 105–6

U   *The Unconsoled* (New York: Vintage International, 1996)

V&H   Allan Vorda and Kim Herzinger, 'An Interview with Kazuo Ishiguro', *Mississippi Review*, 20 (1991), 131–54

Introduction

The child of Japanese parents who moved to Great Britain in 1960, Kazuo Ishiguro identifies the migration from Nagasaki as one of the key turning points of his life, which prefigured some of the themes in his fiction. Ishiguro recalls the first five years of his life in Japan as a happy period that included living in a three-generational household. However, he also notes that the move severed powerful emotional ties he had with his grandfather, who remained for the author an emblem of Japan and Japanese identity; although he believed that his family would reunite in Japan, years passed and it became apparent that his oceanographer father, Shizuo Ishiguro, would accept a permanent position in Great Britain (see especially MJ and KO). Many years after emigration, his father was offered a university position in Japan but turned it down; that incident cemented in Ishiguro's mind that the family would never return to Japan (CW).

Meanwhile, enthusiasm for studying the Japanese language and culture faded as Ishiguro and his elder sisters, Fumiko and Yoko, immersed themselves in English life under the emotional tutelage of their mother, Shizuko Ishiguro. During the family's early years in England, Ishiguro's beloved grandfather died in Japan. Not being present at this important death affected him deeply, although he was not to understand its significance until many years later. Ishiguro explains:

> For me, the creative process has never been about anger or violence, as it is with some people; it's more to do with regret or melancholy. I don't feel I've regretted not having grown up in Japan. That would be absurd. This is the only life I've known. I had a happy childhood, and I've been very happy here. But it's to do with the strong emotional relationships I had in Japan that were suddenly severed at a formative emotional age, particularly with my grandfather. (MJ 23)

In that 1995 interview, the then 40-year-old writer also indicated that, while he does not subscribe to Freudian theory, he believes that this early period of his childhood marked his sense of 'emotional bereavement or emotional deprivation', a sense of 'never having gone back [to Japan and to grandfather], and that there's a whole person [he] was supposed to become [instead]' (MJ 23). In his novels, the main characters search similarly for compensation or consolation from a loss in their lives. Whether the loss is a physical or an emotional one, the characters revisit the traumatic events surrounding their past as they move into an uncertain future. Telling their stories might provide catharsis, by allowing them to reconstruct and perhaps comprehend their loss.

Ishiguro's first two novels, *A Pale View of Hills* (1982) and *An Artist of the Floating World* (1986), are set in Japan, although the author had not returned there since his childhood. The Nobel-prize-winning Japanese author Kenzaburo Oe remarked in a 1989 conversation with Ishiguro that he is deeply impressed by the young writer's 'excellent descriptions of life in Japan, of Japanese buildings and landscapes' in his second novel, and Ishiguro explains that a 'personal, imaginary Japan' remained and developed in his mind: 'All the way through my childhood, I couldn't forget Japan, because I had to prepare myself for returning to it,' but that, eventually, 'one of the real reasons why I turned to writing novels was because I wished to recreate this Japan – put together all these memories, and all these imaginary ideas I had about this landscape which I called Japan' (KO 110). While he emphasizes the imaginary aspects of the contexts in the first two novels, readers nevertheless interpret his novels according to paradigms of his 'oriental' heritage.

With the publication of his third and most acclaimed novel, *The Remains of the Day* (1989), Ishiguro is able to direct readers' attention away from his Japanese origins and focus on his artistic achievements. No longer situated in Japan, this novel examines a period in British history that has as its protagonist a most English caricature – the butler.[1] Still, in early reviews and critical essays, Ishiguro's eloquent and evocative style is a trait that critics identify as integral to his Japanese heritage. Even when *The Remains of the Day* was adapted as a film by Merchant–Ivory Productions in 1993, Ishiguro's ethnicity was frequently noted as one of the defining features of the story's subtle

2

explorations of human relationship against world history.[2] Ishiguro explains: 'The movie casts its own kind of authority. I found myself watching it almost forgetting that I knew the story. In fact, it's a slightly different story that the movie tells. In technical terms, it's a faithful translation, but it's a different work altogether' (SS 105–6). Initially, Harold Pinter was to write the screenplay for *The Remains of the Day*; when Merchant–Ivory Productions resumed control, their own preferred writer, Ruth Prawer Jhabvala, finished the task. The film starred Anthony Hopkins as Stevens and Emma Thompson as Miss Kenton, and it received eight Oscar nominations.

Ishiguro is no novice to visual arts. In 1982 he was commissioned by Channel 4 in Great Britain to write two television dramas, *A Profile of Arthur J. Mason* and *The Gourmet*, which were transmitted in October 1984 and January 1987, respectively.

Within a decade of starting his writing career, literary honours came thick upon Ishiguro. He is the recipient of major literary prizes, including the Winifred Holtby Prize of the Royal Society of Literature for the first novel, the Whitbread Book of the Year Award for the second,[3] the prestigious Booker Prize for *The Remains of the Day*, and the Cheltenham Prize for *The Unconsoled*. He is listed on several 'best of authors' lists, including those by the literary magazine *Granta* and the British Book Marketing Council. In 1995 Ishiguro was decorated by the Queen with the Order of the British Empire (OBE) for service to literature. That same year he received the Premio Scano award for literature in Italy; and, in 1998, he was awarded the Chevalier dans l'Ordre des Arts et Lettres in France for his contribution to literature and culture.

Ishiguro's international status as a writer has evolved relatively quickly. While he does not disavow tendencies in his writing that may strike readers as being particularly Japanese, he indicates that he has always been most interested in writing about universal themes and humanist concerns. His desire to broaden the appeal and themes of his writing may be one of the reasons his fourth novel signifies both a stylistic and substantial departure from the early novels. In *The Unconsoled* (1995), the main character is a famed pianist who arrives in an unnamed European city; his wanderings during the three-day visit do not aspire towards anything resembling real time or real experience, and yet his emotional journey is like the ones undertaken by Ishiguro's other protagonists.

Ishiguro's focus on the emotional and mental configurations of his characters' lives stems from his personal experiences and affinities. He studied in the British school systems when his family first lived in Guildford, Surrey, where he attended Stoughton Primary School and World King County Grammar School; he earned English literature and writing degrees from the University of Kent in 1978 and received a post graduate writing degree from the University of East Anglia in 1980. He has often cited Anton Chekhov, Fydor Dostoevsky, and Franz Kafka as writers who most influenced his technique and vision (see e.g. V&H). He has also expressed admiration for the work of the Latin writers Gabriel García Márquez and Mario Vargas Llosa; the Czech exile writer Milan Kundera; the Irish exile writer Samuel Beckett; and the American exile writer Henry James (V&H 134). (The status of 'exile' is relevant; while Ishiguro has never referred to himself as an 'exile', the theme of this condition certainly applies to many of his concerns in fiction.) Other writers, such as Ford Madox Ford and E. M. Forster, are sometimes invoked by critics who observe such similarities.[4]

On a more personal level, Ishiguro credits writers Angela Carter, Malcolm Bradbury, and Paul Bailey as being significant forces in his own evolving career. Robert McCrum, editorial director at Faber in the 1980s, was among the first to recognize Ishiguro's literary talent, and he published three of Ishiguro's short stories in 1981 in *Introductions 7: Stories by New Writers*. Of Carter, Ishiguro observes that, when he met her in 1979, many of her books were out of print. She had not seen much of Ishiguro's writing, but she eventually became very instrumental as a mentor (CW).

Ishiguro indicates that his career as a full-time writer began around 1982, a period rich in contact with literary figures such as Carter and with future writing possibilities – Ishiguro had recently published his first novel, *A Pale View of Hills*, to much critical acclaim under the editorial guidance of McCrum.

Before 1982 Ishiguro had had his fair share of experimenting with different aesthetic forms. In his early twenties he travelled to the American west coast and British Columbia and kept a writing journal, where he attempted to write fiction. He also once aspired to be a professional musician and tried his hand at song writing; he dismisses those early efforts as 'my kind of intense autobiographical phase . . . [and] wild-purple-prose phase, and then that kind of weird, experimental phase' (DOK 147). (Ishiguro still plays the piano and guitar.) He also draws a distinction between technical experimentation and substantial thematic development in writing fiction.

Ishiguro's social work in Glasgow and London in the early 1980s following his formal education probably shaped his understanding of human awareness and suffering, elements that are present in all of his novels. After publication of his first novel, Ishiguro resumed social work until his writing career became more established. His wife, Lorna MacDougal, is a social worker, and Ishiguro notes that the two of them 'have come across damaged people more frequently than most others have'.[5] Ishiguro's empathies for the disenfranchised and the alienated may also have roots in his childhood awareness and adult experiences of human pain and loss. His subtle indications of hope and human endurance appear in all the novels, however, and, although he has never explicitly indicated the connection, Ishiguro's compassionate attitude towards representing children in his novels may be associated with the birth of his own daughter, Naomi, in 1992.[6]

Importantly, the main characters in Ishiguro's novels are often self-absorbed, but the readers who engage with their stories will find that their quest for consolation is universal. This readerly relationship is especially true of the fourth novel, which is somewhat less ostensibly eloquent and is nearly three times as long as any of the first three. In all of the novels, the author makes an overt attempt to show his protagonists' private penchant for disillusioning themselves as a way to seek comfort from a difficult past. Each of the novels therefore ends on a somewhat odd or confusing note: an awkward cheerfulness permeates each character's consciousness. Ishiguro says, 'I do feel it is somehow pathetic, that kind of cheering up of oneself. But on the other hand, I have a certain kind of admiration for the human capacity to do just that. There's something admirable and courageous about it, even if it seems completely futile.'[7]

This remark is a reminder that literature, like all reflections about human experiences, is an aesthetic form for understanding life: all fictional utterances represent 'homesickness [or the expression of] the urge to be at home everywhere'.[8] As a kind of writer of exile, Ishiguro keenly and sympathetically portrays people searching for their souls and a way to feel at home despite their pain. His own status as an immigrant in the early years of his life probably shaped the emotional exile of his characters.[9] The process of atoning for emotional and physical losses stems deeply from the author's own past, and his novels demonstrate clearly some of the ways he and his characters have discovered solace in an often inconsolable world. In his discussion of what motivates writers, Ishiguro comments, 'I think a lot of [writers] do write out of something that is somewhere deep down and, in fact, it's probably too late ever to resolve it. Writing is a kind of consolation or a therapy' (V&H 151). By extension, reading Ishiguro's novels offers a similar reprieve; as controlled visions set in a fictional context, each of his novels demonstrates how reading and writing – while ostensibly solitary – are extremely social activities that have the ability to link human thoughts and ideas across generations and cultures.

1

Ishiguro as an International Writer

In the mid-1980s, when Ishiguro's writing career was ascending, the British Council's short leaflets introducing British authors had under a photograph of Ishiguro a quote from him: 'I consider myself an international writer.' Over the years, this self-declaration has been reiterated by reviewers and academic critics of his novels, and, while nobody has fully defined what it means exactly to be an 'international writer', the term is a convenient one that addresses both Ishiguro's obvious Japanese ancestry and the kind of broad themes with universal appeal found in his fiction. Salman Rushdie celebrates the latter aspect of Ishiguro's identity when he notes that Ishiguro employs a 'brilliant subversion of the fictional modes' in his discussion of large themes such as 'death, change, pain, and evil'.[1]

In defining the umbrella term 'international writer' a connection between Rushdie and Ishiguro is not an arbitrary one. In 1981 Rushdie was awarded the Booker Prize for *Midnight's Children*, an inventive and sprawling novel about India's independence from Great Britain. Although Ishiguro observes that there are very significant differences between his and Rushdie's works, he credits this moment in Rushdie's career as crucial for his own developing one:

> [Rushdie] had previously been a completely unknown writer. That was a really symbolic moment and then everyone was suddenly looking for other Rushdies. It so happened that around this time I brought out *A Pale View of Hills*. Usually first novels disappear, as you know, without a trace. Yet I received a lot of attention, got lots of coverage, and did a lot of interviews. I know why this was. It was because I had this Japanese face and this Japanese name and it was what was being covered at the time. (V&H 134–5)

7

Eight years later, in 1989, Ishiguro himself won the Booker for *The Remains of the Day*,[2] and he observed that, while the kind of early attention bestowed on him followed from readers' perception of him as an exotic writer (along the lines of their perceptions of writers like Rushdie as well), he believed that he subsequently fought against the very labels that earned him such positive publicity.

If early reviewers admire Japanese attributes of the young writer, they also peg Ishiguro as a foreign writer who just happens to write in the English language. Having lived in Britain since the age of 5 and having spoken and written in the English language since that time, such perceptions are obviously annoying to Ishiguro. At times, he appears exasperated when he explains that the situation and place of his first two novels, *A Pale View of Hills* and *An Artist of the Floating World*, coincide with his Japanese ancestry, but that he is writing works of fiction and not historical texts. Neither is he attempting to capitalize on his exotic status:

> In many ways I felt I was using [Japanese and world] history as a piece of orchestration to bring out my themes. I'm not sure that I ever distorted anything major, but my first priority was not to portray history accurately. Japan and militarism, now these are big, important questions, and it always made me uneasy that my books were being used as a sort of historical text. (DOK 150)

Ishiguro feels a need to explain his fictional inventions and respond to academic perspectives advanced by scholars like Bruce King, who attempts to solidify a concept of what constitutes an 'international writer'. Ishiguro wants the term to denote his literary goals and not his ethnicity alone. King focuses on the latter when he identifies Shiva Naipaul, Rushdie, Buchi Emecheta, Timothy Mo, and Ishiguro as the key figures of 'the new internationalism', and distinguishes such writers from commonwealth, third world, and other ethnic categories. According to King, they 'write about their native lands or the immigrant experience from within the mainstream of British literature'.[3] In Ishiguro's case, however, writing about his native Japan is an act of invention, and he is not speaking from the perspective of an immigrant in either of the first two novels.[4]

King further describes that the new internationalism

reflects the way modern life is characterised by the awareness of new nations, the ease of international travel and communications, the global literary market, the worldwide use of English, and the possibility that assimilation into British culture is no longer the ideal for many who live in England.[5]

This elaboration addresses more clearly Ishiguro's situation as a writer. The kind of global expansion emphasized by King in the above passage describes more vividly Ishiguro's own sensibilities about the meaning of what constitutes 'international'. For the author, ethnicity is not intended as the main subject of any of his books. Rather, Ishiguro's concerns are with the enduring perceptions of his audience from across cultures, particularly with the way they view his handling of important human themes:

> If I were writing a book about British politics in the '60s, there are probably quite a few people in Britain who might be interested in that, but you [the American interviewer] probably wouldn't be, nor would the French people. I do think there are themes or issues that are very urgent locally or to a particular time or place, and I think it's important to address them, but as a novelist, I suppose I'm interested in writing things that will be of interest to people in fifty years' time, a hundred years' time, and to people in lots of different cultures. (DOK 153)

The kind of universal appeal that Ishiguro advocates may be idealistic, but, in his conversation with Kenzaburo Oe, he indicates an awareness of the dangers that certain kinds of 'universalizing' or 'internationalizing' might cause: 'I sometimes worry that writers, being conscious of addressing an international audience, could actually have quite a reverse effect, that something very important in literature might actually die because people water down their artistic instincts' (KO 117). Oe reassures Ishiguro with this remark: 'rather than being an English author or a European author, you are an author who writes in English' (KO 117).

How Ishiguro perceives himself in relation to the international reading community provides a startling contrast to the way critics have subsequently interpreted his novels. Ishiguro explains the discord:

> I was very aware that I had very little knowledge of modern Japan. But still I was writing books set in Japan, or supposedly set in Japan.

9

My very lack of authority and lack of knowledge about Japan, I think, forced me into a position of using my imagination, and also of thinking of myself as a kind of homeless writer. I had no obvious social role, because I wasn't a very English Englishman, and I wasn't a very Japanese Japanese either. (KO 115)

In identifying Ishiguro as 'an author who writes in English', Oe responds to the critical views that stereotype Ishiguro's writing, to good and ill effects. Oe refers to Edward Said's polemical stance that 'orientalism' has to do with how white Europeans construct a notion of what is 'oriental' or derives from the 'Orient'.[6] Notably, such constructions are usually erroneous and serve instead to validate gross generalizations one culture makes about another, usually subordinate, one. Indeed, Ishiguro's first two novels, set in Japan, are frequently described by readers as having quiet, peaceful, delicate, subtle qualities resonant with Japanese culture, both in the substance of the stories and the author's evocation of their tales. While not necessarily pejorative, these somewhat patronizing terms situate Ishiguro's Japanese ancestry as the main source of his writing and disregard the author's own claims that what he writes about Japan is largely invented or produced by his active imagination. And, more importantly, he uses Japan as a starting point to orchestrate crucial themes, such as alienation and suffering; he is not one Japanese speaking for all Japanese about Japan (GM 342).

Even Bruce King's earnest stance about the 'new international-alism' uses orientalist language to describe Ishiguro's writing style; such emphasis on the author's Asian ancestry distracts from the large human themes important to Ishiguro:

His instincts are for the nuanced, the understated, elegant but significant gesture, similar to the deft brushwork of Japanese paintings. While Ishiguro can make comedy of the extremes of Oriental manners, his novels require us to understand by indirec-tion, by analogy with the way Japanese conversations move politely around the matter at issue.[7]

Not surprisingly, the subject matter of Ishiguro's first two novels may lend itself to the above orientalist analysis, but King has difficulty analysing Ishiguro's third, ostensibly not Japanese, novel, *The Remains of the Day*, against the same critical description.[8]

Some academic essays on Ishiguro's novels use a paradigm based on the author's Asian heritage to explain or interpret stylistic matters of his writing. Most notably, Gregory Mason's striking essay on the influences of Japanese cinema in the first two novels confirms subsequent sentiments that the subject of Ishiguro's concerns is rooted in efforts 'to create a distinctively personal style of unusual resonance and subtlety' that is mostly related to his being Asian.[9] Less effective in establishing Ishiguro's unique literary style is John Rothfork's essay on Zen comedy, which offers a way to analyse *The Remains of the Day* by 'using comparative religion and philosophy to provide key terms and concepts to comprehend non-Western identity, motives and values'.[10] Other post-colonial or cultural examinations of Ishiguro's novels include essays by Susie O'Brien, who discusses, among other important themes, the 'positive diversity' of the emerging multiculturalism of British fiction;[11] and by Meera Tamaya, who notices that Ishiguro creates a post-colonial figure in Stevens 'with the delicate economy of a sketch by [Japanese painter] Hokusai'.[12] Despite Ishiguro's exasperation with such stereotyping of his ethnicity as one element of being an international writer, the literary situation in Britain in the 1980s and 1990s confirmed a movement towards multiculturalism and a celebration of cultural diversity. In other words, Ishiguro's emergence as a writer coincided with an atmosphere that highlighted his role as a bicultural author. If readers first notice that Ishiguro is of Japanese ancestry and find relevant cultural paradigms to approach his fiction, it does not escape their attention that he is a writer who writes sensibly and insightfully about grand human concerns as well. It is then only a matter of time until Ishiguro is received more generally as 'an author who writes in English' and whose audience and subject matter are international in scope and content as well.

In a chapter whose title pays tribute to Ishiguro, 'Artists of the Floating World', Malcolm Bradbury writes, 'The British fiction of the Eighties felt less like the writing of a common culture than of a multiplying body of cultures, adding to the mixed fund of myths, the surging sea of stories, and extending and varying the prevailing notions of what the British novel might be.'[13] Bradbury draws up a list of writers in Britain with international roots or affiliations; along with most writers of Irish origins, he includes Salman Rushdie (India), Adam Zameenzad (Pakistan), Timothy Mo (Hong Kong), Ben Okri (Nigeria), Caryl Phillips (St Kitts in the Caribbean), and Ishiguro (Japan).[14]

The 'new spirit of ethnic and stylistic multiculturalism that has been widening the vision and range of... the British novel', as described by Bradbury, is the situation in which Ishiguro's writing gained prominence.[15] In his quest for 'the fabled London literary life' of the 1990s, Jonathan Wilson also makes this observation: 'Ishiguro does occupy a singular place in British writing: he is neither native-born nor a descendant of the Old Empire, and thus stands outside the peculiarly charged and ambivalent relationship between the ex-colonies and Britain.'[16] Such a sense of 'homelessness' in situating Ishiguro among writers of British fiction may therefore have both positive and negative implications: what might be a reference point for approaching Ishiguro's writing? Bradbury adds that, in contrast to Rushdie's fiction, which depicts 'the fragmentation, violence and disorder of a multi-cultural but incoherent Britain, ruled by a "'Mrs Torture'"', Ishiguro's fiction marries 'British with other forms of fiction to create an international, late-modern fictional voice that is . . . larger than any individual culture'.[17] Seen, therefore, as a conglomerate of voices and concerns, the novel written by an international writer such as Ishiguro is historically situated, culturally rich, and humanistically oriented, even if the writer's own sensibilities continue to shift with his or her own sense of 'the way history is moving' (KO 119). In both form and content, Ishiguro's writing certainly embodies the above characteristics.

However, Ishiguro is wary of labels and such forms of group identification among writers, even at the risk of appearing lost or 'homeless' among the crowds. He aligns with but refuses to be placed as a 'group' among contemporary writers such as Ian McEwan, William Boyd, Martin Amis, Julian Barnes, Graham Swift, and Ann Beattie, all writers he otherwise admires and who seem to share a contemporary view that 'Britain is not the center of the universe' (V&H 139). A common theme of decentering British authority may unite such writers, but their individual visions and styles should set them apart, according to Ishiguro. For his part, Ishiguro, the writer with Japanese origins, is not writing about his own immigrant experiences in Great

Britain, as Bruce King would have it; in *The Remains of the Day*, for instance, Ishiguro says that he actually sets out to 'rework a particular myth about a certain kind of mythical England' (V&H 139). A similar demystifiying of Japanese culture following the atomic war may be said to occur in Ishiguro's first two novels, but readers do well to remember the author's own caution that he is primarily concerned with the emotional impact that such world events had on individual lives. More importantly, his novels are not intended as accurate and objective historical texts.

Regarded as imaginative works, Ishiguro's novels have an inexplicable power to express the emotional conditions of people undergoing intense experiences related to recognizable world events. Though not viewed as texts with veritable historical objectivity, the fiction still achieves a compelling reader's response like the one that Nobel-prize-winning author Nadine Gordimer discusses:

> If you want to read the facts of the retreat from Moscow in 1812, you may read a history book; if you want to know what war is like and how people of a certain time and background dealt with it as their personal situation, you must read *War and Peace*.[18]

While it is difficult to declare that a novel like *A Pale View of Hills* is *not* a truthful account of post-war Nagasaki, it is more likely that the novel *is* a faithful imaginative rendering of the emotional life of one woman remembering a tumultuous time in her private life set in the charged atmosphere of post-atomic warfare. By focusing on the emotional turmoil of his protagonist's *personal situation* against the orchestrated background of nuclear devastation, Ishiguro can appeal to a wide audience. Seen as polemical and charged primarily because of universal agreement that atomic warfare is painfully destructive, the novel would have no difficulty finding international readership in Japan, Britain, America, or any of the other twelve nations into whose language this novel was translated.[19]

Ishiguro does not regard his novels as academic exercises; neither does he wish to write without 'communicating a vision' (V&H 149). The main point of his writing is to rework or to undermine certain ideals or mythologies structuring individuals, communities, or their nations, mainly in efforts to regard the impact of such visions on people's actual lives. Ishiguro is not out to baffle, intellectualize, trivialize, or otherwise appropriate real human pain and happiness for its own sake, but he seeks to find new ways of expressing these in a discourse of fiction (V&H 144).[20] Such discourse is social in that the writer presents ethical dilemmas confronting his characters and asks readers to examine the life strategies explored in the fiction. Inherently universal, such concerns are also international in scope and may endure the historical times and people that Ishiguro envisions.

A key to understanding Ishiguro's novels lies in the author's own concerns with his perceived audience of readers. Claiming that 'I have to be international [in my writing]', Ishiguro also cautions against the way 'people have to sacrifice many things that make their culture unique and, in fact, make their art and culture mean something [but in that process end up contributing] to this meaningless blanket' (KO 119). Aware that overly determining any particular historical situation may eradicate a truth that all history and people change in the course of time, Ishiguro is also concerned with how to incorporate that knowledge of change and inconstancy in his novels. In other words, his characters must be realistically portrayed according to the contexts of their given situations, but their awareness of that situation must be seen as undergoing transformation conducive to the way actual people indeed do change. Can people really be aware of being both central and peripheral to their own stories? Furthermore, how can the compression of their narrated tales in the space of a literary text manage such dual roles? A closer look at Ishiguro's narrative strategies will establish some possible answers.

2

Reading the Novels

After the publication of his second novel, *An Artist of the Floating World*, Ishiguro said that he was exploring how his first-person narrators used 'the language of self-deception and self-protection' (GM 337) to convey their life stories. On the surface, Ishiguro's protagonists appear as 'self-conscious narrators' who are distinctly aware of themselves as writers of their own stories; as they are observing or remembering their lives, they also comment selectively on *how* they are 'writing, thinking, speaking, or "reflecting"' that life.[1] The narrator's dual roles of reading significance into and then documenting the details of that life are linked to a particular kind of self-deception that interested Ishiguro. He sympathizes with how the deception signifies a character's guarding against emotional injury or harm; accordingly, an actual reader could identify with the ethical dilemmas forcing the characters into forms of simultaneous deception and protection.

In his first two novels, characters attempt to rebuild their lives following one of the century's worst calamities upon their society, the bombings of Hiroshima and Nagasaki. Ishiguro uses the historical situation to explore his characters' emotions. In manifesting self-dignity, his characters turn inward for courage to speak about their lives years, even decades, later when they are facing an important turning point in their own or their family's lives. In *The Remains of the Day*, Stevens's position as butler compels an economy of speaking as well. To voice one's emotions at all times would appear out of character for these narrators, for silence is as much an aspect of their stories as the words that they eventually utter. People 'manage reality by their constructions', writes postmodern critic Ihab Hassan, and silence as one form of such a construction 'fills the extreme

15

states of the mind – void, madness, outrage, ecstasy, mystic trance – when ordinary discourse ceases to carry the burden of meaning'.[2]

Such gaps – such silences filling the void – in the narrators' stories signal an important reading strategy crucial to Ishiguro's development of his characters. How Ishiguro employs gaps to unveil his characters' pain of suffering approximates the artistic effect described by social critic David B. Morris:

> Writers can open up the interior or private life of a character in ways often difficult or impossible outside of texts, revealing a personal side of affliction that we rarely see. Moreover, they can infuse the voices of suffering with an unusual power to move emotion and compel attention. In both ways, writers create the occasion for an empathetic reader-response that . . . holds a power to address, or even reverse, the inherent pressure within affliction toward isolation and silence.[3]

Ishiguro's concerns with how his characters read into and then interpret their life stories reflect those shared by critics who engage in an aesthetic theory of reading literary texts; that is, Ishiguro establishes the potential for 'an empathetic reader-response' between his characters and his readers. Such critics, variously engaged in an 'aesthetic of reception' or 'reader-response' forms of criticism, agree on this relationship that literary texts can establish with their readers:

> Every time a human being reaches out, across, or by means of symbols to the world, he reenacts the principles that define that mingling of self and other, the creative and relational quality of all our experience, not the least the writing and reading of literature.[4]

How his characters come to a realization of the forces of their lives and how they rewrite these details to suit their narratives are as important to Ishiguro as the way his actual readers apprehend their own interpretive process while reading his novels.[5]

Seen as providing a link between author and reader, novels like Ishiguro's can produce a state of consciousness that interacts with the reading and the writing of that novel's situation. Ishiguro's characters emerge in relatively simplistic situations but are revealed to be carrying with them complicated states of being. Through Ishiguro's evocative narrative style, the richness of their crises may be examined and have, as a result, an important didactic function for understanding human emotion. Reader-response theory may prove helpful in such instances of interpretation, since its paradigm fits with Ishiguro's portrayals of the psyches of his characters responding to historical and personal forces in their lives.

According to reader-response theorists, two distinct literary poles are discerned as a first step towards unravelling a writer's narrative strategy: an *artistic* one that is 'the text created by the author' and an *aesthetic* one that is 'the realization accomplished by the reader'.[6] The way the poles might converge to produce a vital situation requires from the reader a 'game of the imagination';[7] how an artistic text gives life to an aesthetic experience further depends on an author's careful rendering of what to include and what to leave out of the narrator's tale. If Ishiguro's narrators both lie and comfort themselves in the same breath, what they do not tell is as dynamic as what they reveal, according to the way that such gaps in storytelling produce 'the inexhaustibility of [meaning within] the text'.[8] How conscious are the narrators of their own efforts to reveal, conceal, evade, and protect? Or, in a related query, how does Ishiguro's artistic manipulation render their silence as provocative as the words they do utter?

A narrative strategy of using memory and hindsight characterizes the stories recounted by Etsuko in *A Pale View of Hills*, and Masuji Ono in *An Artist of the Floating World*. Both seem careful about not overburdening their listeners with superfluous details; as their pasts emerge more vividly, despite their own a-chronological approach, it is clearer that careful reflection on the narrators' parts is a guise for purposeful deflection of injurious details. Seen first as offering simple stories on the surface, the narrators also reveal how deeply their self-estrangement runs. Critic Reed Way Dasenbrock notes that, as we readers 'actually interpret, we encounter anomalies, sentences that don't seem to agree with what we hold true', because of the narrator's clever uses of language.[9] A reader's realization of such an aesthetic effect arises directly from Ishiguro's literary method: in order to create an emotional atmosphere where honesty and dishonesty of self-revelation might be discerned, Ishiguro combines narrative technique with a concern for human psychology, both for his characters who read and write their tales *and* for his actual readers. How does Ishiguro's development of his narrators' duplicitous uses of language coincide with the way people such as Etsuko and Ono might find a stable existence following their nation's nuclear devastation?

After publication of *The Remains of the Day*, Ishiguro again emphasized the necessity of his narrator's 'suppression of emotion' and how the language of that novel shows that the main character Stevens is 'actually hiding from what is perhaps the scariest arena in life, which is the emotional arena' (V&H 142). By privileging this elusive arena of human experience as a theme and motive for the novel, Ishiguro highlights the techniques people use either to uncover or further to suppress their emotions, particularly the way that these emotions are prompted by memory. Importantly, the novels all have relatively clear time frames of past and present, but, as the narrators delve into their memories, these two frames become complicated, and, at times, distorted by emotion. In fact, what separates past from present is a volatile divide; their narrations attempt to mollify the eruptions.

Subsequently, all of the novels depend on these recognizable temporal orders: anticipation, flashback, and discordance, with the last term signalling emotional distress.[10] When Etsuko, Ono, Stevens, and Ryder of the novels begin their respective narrations, they anticipate a physical event that serves as a driving force for their speaking; as they move their stories into the past with the benefit or deficiency of memory, they begin to reveal incongruities in their stories. The stories they tell and the way they tell them seem not always to coincide. How purposeful or how innocent are their eventual narrations?

The selective narration presented in the novels each reveals significant aspects of the particular character's crisis; each narrator is in effect *writing* his or her own story along an emotional course to be tracked by a reader or listener who will bear witness to the tales.[11] To construct their stories according to this writer–reader paradigm, the narrators find themselves both at the centre and at the margins of their own stories: as careful readers of their own lives, they move away from a painful version, in order to lure another interested listener–reader to

18

their tale. This complex rendering of the narrator's conscious-ness and his or her motivation for speaking requires a phenomenological effort that reader–response critic Georges Poulet identifies as a 'strange displacement [of the narrator] by the work' occurring.[12] Eventually, the narrators come to believe in what they have created as the *verité de l'histoire* they had been after all along.[13] So, persuaded by their own conviction of truth, the narrators reveal their eventual ease with self-deception to achieve a self-comforting or self-protecting condition.

In establishing motive for the narrators' duplicity, it is helpful to examine Ishiguro's self-deceiving and self-protecting narrators as historically constituted subjects; a useful postmodern assess-ment includes seeing these subjects as 'unfixed, unsatisfied' entities who are 'not a unity, not autonomous, but a process, perpetually in construction, perpetually contradictory, perpetu-ally open to change'.[14] Like actual writers who appropriate useful ideas from linguistic and personality theories to present their characters, the fictional narrators of these novels cunningly employ similar strategies to present their best self-portrait possible. Like actual people who must face the entanglements wrought upon them either by historical circumstances or their own choices, the narrators show a human propensity and need for consolation. All of these forces add another emotional layer to the aesthetic effect generated by Ishiguro's artistic construction of their tales.

To achieve the effects of both their suffering and their need for consolation, Ishiguro's narrators split into two distinct roles. Two levels of narrative voice can be distinguished from the one speaking in each of the novels: an 'extradiegetic' narrator is '"above" or superior to the story he narrates' and a 'homodiegetic' narrator 'takes part in [the story]'.[15] Each level is determined by the temporal situation manipulated by the narrator. Thus, when Etsuko moves into a past description of her life in Nagasaki, she creates an effect of being 'above' the story she narrates, until she lets slip the fact that she is still very much deeply involved in the emotional turmoil of that period; her own confusion of being either above or within the story adds to the tumultuous sense of her emotions during that volatile period of her life.

19

Although his novels refer to realistic situations and characters, Ishiguro is the first to remind his readers that he is writing fiction, and, therefore, achieves aesthetic effects by envisioning how people manage their lives along with the delusions and truths that form them. In having Etsuko and Ono reconstruct their life stories in post-war Japanese society, Ishiguro says, 'I am not essentially concerned with a realist purpose in writing. I just invent a Japan which serves my needs. And I put that Japan together out of little scraps, out of memories, out of speculation, out of imagination' (GM 341). Aware of his status as a 'non-English, non-white writer in British society', Ishiguro is regarded by critics in Britain and abroad as both insider and outsider, as well as reader and writer of the cultures he explores in his literature.[16] The contexts found in Ishiguro's fiction bear resemblance to real places and times, but the author emphatically notes that what he strives for in his work is the representation of human emotions and experiences in an accessible language; such realistic references as the history of either Japan or Britain are secondary to the emotional lives of his protagonists, as noted in the previous chapter of this book.

Reader–response critics also describe a 'horizon of expectation' that exists for characters and offers a useful means for assessing their culpability in speaking lies and half-truths; the term 'implies that the condition of existence of a consciousness is not available to this consciousness in a conscious mode, just as, in a perception, conscious attention is possible only upon a background, or horizon, of distraction'.[17] In other words, if their portraits appear cunning, perhaps the narrators remain unaware of the power of the language they have used to tell their stories. Unable to regard all the forces of their past and present – or unable to manipulate the horizon of their own stories without finally revealing their deception – they produce what reader-response critic Hans Robert Jauss describes as 'stories in which the truth of life continually denies the mendacious character of poetic fiction'.[18] In noting how Ishiguro's narrators seem to seek truth but then persistently evade it, or retell versions of that truth in more ostensibly comforting ways, readers subsequently gain awareness of how his fiction reveals more accurate aspects of human efforts of consolation: not always knowing what to seek, his narrators stumble through a life they do not always understand. In other words, strangely aware and unaware of the way their lives have turned out, the narrators' consciousness of events and their significance offers an unusually dynamic way of examining truth-making in fictional texts. Or, how might we consider the way Ishiguro's *fiction* offers the 'truth of life' to readers who discover that such a condition persistently evades its own narrators?

Out of his own memories, speculation, and imagination, Ishiguro produces conditions not always of physical reality but those related to people's sense of 'emotional bereavement or emotional deprivation', including in many ways, the author's own (MJ 21). Finding a way to speak about personal pain is immensely difficult, as these narrators show, and their eloquence may actually betray their struggle to find a way. Ishiguro's literary style therefore may be characterized best as deeply involved in developing this kind of social discourse of the novel:

> a prose writer can distance himself from the language of his own work, while at the same time distancing himself, in varying degrees, from the different layers and aspects of the work. He can make use of language without wholly giving himself up to it, he may treat it as semi-alien or completely alien to himself, while compelling language ultimately to serve all his own intentions.[19]

Ishiguro develops his broad concerns for the way people seek truth in their lives, but who then find multiple ways of dismantling access to it, because of the painfulness of truth itself. In effect, what is most familiar to them is also most alien; perhaps a language of fiction can capture these two senses of finding ways to express an ambivalent emotional state. Provocatively, through a concealment of pain, the narrators also reveal their fear of revelation and knowledge of their lives; language is both expiation and condemnation for those who begin a narrative act leading to self-awareness.

Familiar themes and subjects therefore receive innovative consideration from Ishiguro, since ordinary everyday objects might link humans to deeper recesses of their being. In discussing some of the artistic influences found in Ishiguro's first two novels, Gregory Mason notes that the author's images of a remembered Japan are in fact derived from Japanese cinema. The film-maker Yasujiro Ozu's emphasis on the genre

21

shomin-geki, or domestic drama, seems to have an important effect on Ishiguro, according to Mason.[20] Its concerns with the representation of ordinary, 'normal', people may be particularly appealing to Ishiguro, whose works are filled with situations that examine the ideals and the disappointments of home life. Indeed, all four of his novels contain a domestic focus, whether of Etsuko's early married life in Japan and eventual exile into the empty house in Britain, Ono's troubled relationships with his two daughters in the war-ravished and once-grand home in post-war Japan, Stevens's beleaguered service as butler to a once-great lord and his eventual displacement into the service of a wealthy American in the same great estate, or, in *The Unconsoled*, of Ryder's confusion of a family life he vaguely remembers as he tours in an oddly familiar city.

Themes of self, family, and nation recur in all of Ishiguro's novels. Daily or regular relationships between people, particularly between parents and their children or between teachers and their pupils, provide a significant focus in all of the novels and offer a starting point for his parables; kinship scenes often involve conflict, especially across generations, as people strive to communicate their ideals and their values to relatives. Usually, failure of communication stems from failed attempts to be tactful or courageous under unusual circumstances, such as the promoting of family understanding, the rebuilding of a war-torn society, or the healing of a divided community. Even so, a human need to suppress emotion and an inability to proclaim pain often direct the way the characters relate to one another.

Across generations, kinship relations frequently mirror societal ones; what individual families struggle against may be discovered in the kinds of forces found in their particular cultural contexts. Etsuko's husband and father-in-law engage in controlled discussions of the divide within Japan following the surrender; similarly, exchanges between Ono and his sons-in-law and their peers show the latter's resentment of their imperialist-influenced elders. Stevens has a strained, if polite, relationship with his father, who was a renowned butler in his own day. And, Boris – who may or may not be Ryder's son – struggles for attention from his mother and Ryder in what may be best described as a dysfunctional household.

Human relationships in Ishiguro's novels reveal discord or deeply discouraging conditions of family life (and, by extension, of community life), although Ishiguro's portrayals may be regarded less as a critical or cynical view of domestic life than as an effort to show the real difficulties involved in maintaining civility under domestic circumstances. Etsuko's disillusionment with married life in Japan is recounted through her remembrances of another woman, Sachiko, who had a difficult time maintaining intimacy with other people. The manner in which Sachiko's daughter suffers as a result of her mother's failed relationships makes it possible for Etsuko, years later, to remember what might have precipitated her own daughter's suicide in England. Less enigmatic, but no less telling, is the way Ono is unable to relate to his own daughters after the war has killed his wife and son (whose deaths are mentioned only in passing) – he recounts the way they would corner him in conversations, even though he himself seems to present evidence to support their mistrust of him. Stevens's love interest, the former Miss Kenton, relates to him some of the sorrows attendant to her life as Mrs Benn when she conveys to him her own regret at their lost opportunities for love. By contrast, Ryder's lack of awareness of life with Sophie and her son, Boris, suggests his preference for an artistic existence as opposed to the shackles of domesticity represented by his neglected 'family'.

Ishiguro notes that, with each successive work, he was hoping to capture the elusiveness of human consciousness and the way people justify losses and failures. After publication of *The Unconsoled*, Ishiguro said that he 'was trying to leave behind' a particular way of conveying his character's situation, 'that relatively tranquil atmosphere on the surface with frustrations bubbling underneath' (MJ 22). The fourth novel, therefore, represents a stylistic departure for Ishiguro. If a poignant, even elegiac, mood pervades the first three novels, humour and an improvisation of mood characterize the fourth. Comic situations abound in the early novels, as well, and Ishiguro presents his characters in a variety of situations. He mixes different moods in his novels, from the comic to the tragic, from the sombre to the absurd. Each of his novels supports Ishiguro's contention that, though his characters fail at something essential in their lives, they eventually find the momentum and energy to keep moving forward. The futility of his characters' plights, coupled with their ability to remain forward-looking, adds a poignant dimension to the author's view of the world.

Ishiguro's novels all employ a first-person, seemingly self-conscious, narrating strategy. Consequently, the stories told by each may be open to charges of unreliable points of view or biased presentation. If the narrators are purposely deceiving their readers or listeners, some of the deception may be overlooked, given their eloquent manner of speaking. The solemn tone of the first two novels, in particular, suggests that the narrators are struggling to remember as best they can. Indeed, both Etsuko and Ono – and, to a degree, Stevens and Ryder – all confess to a memory that may be flawed or tainted by the passage of time. Their own insistence that what they are remembering may be a piece of a larger picture on the whole gains a reader's trust, for who has not at times embellished a detail or unknowingly left out a small piece of information? Though a reader may suspect the narrator's deception, their open admission of real human flaws gains a reader's empathy. The narrators are human in that they are vulnerable.

Because each of the main characters also suffers tremendous losses of both personal and professional kinds, readers may gain additional empathy for them. Readers learn early on of the death of Etsuko's daughter by suicide, the deaths of Ono's wife and son, as well as his forced resignation as artist, Stevens's loss of Miss Kenton as the possible love of his life as well as loss of his father, and Ryder's dislocated or lost family. Each of the storytellers is ostensibly working through the pain of his or her losses through the process of remembering and recording, and part of the process includes inducting witnesses into the tales. Their social suffering may arise from a personal situation, but their stories do not emphasize somatic or physical pain so much as they reveal the fragmentation caused by psychological and spiritual forms of suffering.[21] The cathartic effect sought by the narrators, therefore, infuses their stories with a realism that softens the edges of their 'deception'. If their narratives are riddled with inconsistencies or awkward insistence, this may be the result of a memory that is also struggling to bring to the surface painful events and to find a language that can adequately express the unending trauma of their affliction.

All the narrators describe important aspects of experiences in order to understand their effect as they see the end of their lives looming. They are engaged in the difficulty of understanding life in order to comfort themselves, even if they must lie in order to discover such 'truth' of satisfaction. Unlike autobiographical works, which strive to show discernible beginnings, middles, and ends through retrospection, Ishiguro's novels instead reveal how such linear or chronological unfolding proves detrimental to expressing the emotional substance of the narrators' accounts. Often, memories are not ordered in logical fashion, and ambiguous territory such as desires or involuntary memory may be more indicative of how people are inspired to convey their stories. Of the first three novels, Ishiguro seems aware of these gaps and the limitations of linearity and truthful representation when he notes that 'I was interested in how people lie to themselves just to make things palatable, to make a sense of yourself bearable. We all dignify our failures a little bit, and make the best of our successes. I was interested in how someone settles on a picture of himself and his life' (MJ 23). The odd self-satisfying moment at the end of each of his novels may reveal some of the dissonance between what actually occurred in the narrator's life with what he or she comes to regard as an acceptable version. Speaking about the events may allow people both to deceive and to protect themselves. Linking this human strategy of survival to a narrative technique, Ishiguro says:

> To combat complacency, I suppose I'm always trying to remind myself in my writing that while we may be very pleased with ourselves, we may look back with a different perspective, and see we may have acted out of cowardice and failure of vision. What I'm interested in is not the actual fact that my characters have done things they later regret. I'm interested in how they come to terms with it.[22]

Speaking about their lives when they are old or when they can no longer eradicate old patterns for living, Ishiguro's narrators essentially fictionalize their lives by reading and writing their own significance.

Writing on *An Artist of the Floating World*, Kathryn Morton also comments on how Ishiguro 'stretches the reader's awareness, teaching him to read more perceptively'.[23] If the characters manage to emerge as deceptive yet sympathetic, these over-

25

lapping qualities compel the reader to sort out what is the fact of their suffering and what they restrain from revealing. Ishiguro expects his readers to participate in the narrators' painful reconstruction of their failed lives. In the first three novels, expressing the situation or historical context demands a narrator's emotional restraint for understating the worst aspects of an experience, and a careful reader must note where ellipses or gaps in the narrators' stories occur. Ishiguro adeptly portrays the turmoil of his characters' situations in elegantly evocative discourse; their remembered accounts show what difficulty they have in owning up to a view of their actions and decisions. If they suffer privately, their language carries the implications of suffering into social and ethical arenas. A compassionate novelist, Ishiguro carefully develops the silent anguish of people who suffer, and he gives them voice for locating solace.

3

Narrative and Memory: *A Pale View of Hills*

Life . . . can be lived with integrity only if death is already accepted as inseparable from it.[1]

Etsuko, the narrator of Ishiguro's first novel, adopts an unusually quiet tone when speaking about her past. She is living in England when she narrates the period shortly after the bombing of Nagasaki. Etsuko's memories are precipitated by her second daughter Niki's spring visit, and she speaks in an oddly calm voice about events that are revealed to have had devastating personal and historical consequences.[2] When the novel begins, the reader learns that Etsuko's eldest daughter, Keiko, had been living estranged from the family for over six years when she was found dead in her Manchester rooms, an apparent suicide by hanging. During Niki's visit, Etsuko is reminded of a woman named Sachiko and her young and disturbed daughter, Mariko, who had lived near her in Nagasaki during the period of the city's reconstruction. The circumstances of Niki's visit appear pleasant enough, but Etsuko admits that 'although we never dwelt long on the subject of Keiko's death, it was never far away, hovering over us whenever we talked' (*PVH* 10).

As the narrative evolves and as details become paradoxically more clear and murky, the reader discovers that Etsuko remembers the 'friendship [of] no more than a matter of some several weeks one summer many years ago' (*PVH* 11) in order to explain to herself what happened to Keiko. More specifically, the details of Sachiko's life seem to mirror and to foreshadow aspects of Etsuko's own, and her return to this period initially seems to help her mourn for Keiko.

27

In his aesthetic of reception theory, Georges Poulet describes a process by which people split into two distinct selves as they read into or reread aspects of a significant story: 'Withdrawn in some recess of myself, do I then silently witness this dispossession? Do I derive from it some comfort, or on the contrary, a kind of anguish?'[3] Poulet's distinction of a self that experiences life and an 'other' self that interprets those experiences provides a useful paradigm for understanding Etsuko's dual roles in her own narrative; it also helps a reader understand how Etsuko can appear so self-possessed and calm when speaking about such tragic events as her daughter's death and her country's atomic devastation. In effect, her story is an effort to reread and rewrite aspects of her own understanding of life. Like the actual reader who witnesses the unfolding of her story through the time frames and situations she touches upon, Etsuko herself is a kind of reader who begins a process of self-understanding that requires that she simultaneously distances herself from and plunges herself into a murky past. In effect, she is composed of the two halves described by Poulet: Etsuko's dispossession of an anguished self is an attempt at recovering comfort for her other self. Another way of examining this motif of split selves for Etsuko's role as a mother is to consider that she is putting her first daughter to rest in her memory, so that she may focus on her remaining daughter.

As Etsuko narrates the events of the past and present, she occasionally stops herself to assess the reliability of her memory; perhaps, in doing so, she determines whether she derives comfort or anguish from their examination. Early on, she warns herself and her listener that, 'It is possible that my memory of these events will have grown hazy with time, that things did not happen in quite the way they come back to me today' (PVH 41). Later, after many stories have been told, Etsuko again repeats, 'Memory, I realize, can be an unreliable thing; often it is heavily coloured by the circumstances in which one remembers, and no doubt this applies to certain of the recollections I have gathered here' (PVH 156). In these instances, Etsuko observes the limitations of her memory, and she recalls distinctly an 'eerie spell' (PVH 41) or a 'premonition' (PVH 156) that surrounds the remembrances of those events. At other times, she hints at supernatural possibilities or refers to events or people in both past and present whose significance she leaves unexplained. The calm tone she has used throughout begins to show through, and the reader realizes that Etsuko may be suppressing or hiding from the painful facts of that period. Her narrative only appears lucidly constructed, despite her own misgivings about a flawed memory, but it is riddled with evasions of more painful truths about her life and her daughter's death. Apparitions haunt her memories and suggest an unsettled atmosphere. The gaps in her telling indicate what directions her memory is headed.

Gregory Mason identifies Ishiguro's portrayal of Etsuko's emotional state as an expression of what the Japanese call *mono no aware*, a term that roughly translates into 'the sadness of things' or 'sensitivity to things'.[4] Memory of the dead, for instance, is tied to an awareness of life's ephemeral or transient qualities. As an attribute of her narrative, *mono no aware* also describes Etsuko's awareness of what is real in terms of her feelings and what in relation to historical or objective reality. When a person undertakes the quest towards comprehension, such sensitivity also contributes to a 'knowledge of the impossibility of knowing [that] precedes the act of consciousness that tries to reach it'.[5] Already deeply aware that the return to her past will not bring back her dead daughter, Etsuko is nevertheless compelled to mend her understanding of how events evolved. That stories require an act of interpretive reconstruction that can produce distinct forms of knowing and not-knowing is relevant to Etsuko's narrative role.[6] Unable to fathom the truth of her daughter's suicide, she still desires to appease her need to know; sadly, she also understands that whatever she learns of Keiko's reasons for choosing death will not offer genuine solace.

As Etsuko observes Sachiko and Mariko, she notices that the daughter shows troubling signs of being neglected: Mariko seems withdrawn and inattentive. Although she reaches out to Mariko, Etsuko realizes even then that her gestures are useless and that Mariko harbours deeply rooted resentments against her mother and other people. Etsuko makes these observations from the perspective of hindsight, because she does not understand their significance or relevance to herself until years later in England. Because Etsuko is pregnant with her first child (Keiko) at the time of this unusual friendship with Sachiko, she fears that her own 'misgiving about motherhood' (*PVH* 17) will be confirmed. Already aware of Keiko's unhappy life and death, the reader understands that Etsuko's misgivings in the past become realized even before the novel begins. Ishiguro is adept at moving seamlessly across past, present, and future events, because the events of the different periods all contribute to the sad consequences of Etsuko's life and Keiko's death.[7]

As the friendship between the two women unfolds from Etsuko's memory, the reader begins to suspect that Sachiko may be a figment of Etsuko's imagination and that the death of her own grown daughter Keiko may have inspired the creation of a fictive friendship from the past. Indeed, Etsuko herself seems to confuse her memories of Sachiko with characteristics that are her own. For instance, early on in the novel, Etsuko remembers that Sachiko's arrival in the area sparked interest and gossip; she recounts overhearing two women talking about the newcomer at the tram stop: 'They discussed for a while her "American friend" ... [and] then the woman spoke again of how unfriendly the stranger [i.e. Sachiko] had been to her that morning' (*PVH* 13). Etsuko follows this observation with an explanation, 'It was never my intention to appear unfriendly, but it was probably true that I made no special effort to seem otherwise' (*PVH* 13). Although Etsuko begins speaking about an event concerning Sachiko, she reacts as if the women at the tram stop had been speaking about her, and this confusion causes the reader to reconsider the connection Etsuko makes between herself and Sachiko; it is as if she has literally split into two people in this memory. Despite the similarities between the two women, the reader also understands that Etsuko is remembering a woman who may have been more like herself than she realized at the time. Poulet's theory of the split selves has particular resonance in this scene, because Etsuko's perception of herself is entwined with her present memory of Sachiko; how Etsuko *reads* Sachiko's significance in the present moment will reveal what she had suppressed about her own relationship with her daughter Keiko.

Another similar confusion of identities appears later in the novel when Etsuko appears to be having a conversation with Mariko. As the dialogue evolves, it appears as if Etsuko is talking to her own daughter Keiko on the eve of their eventual departure from Japan. Rather than provide a continuous record of events between her and Sachiko's family, Etsuko seems to be associating the experiences of her friend with her own. Etsuko's remembrances therefore seem to be more random than she is presenting them; because subsequent events remembered by her do not help explain previous ones, the reader can be confused by the narrator's motives. When readers supply missing links to gaps in a story, they enact a process similar to one facing the writer as he or she is constructing the story: writers or their fabricators 'create an intricate web of character and circumstance that will "motivate" the scene or push it to a revealing conclusion'.[8] Ishiguro creating Etsuko's story, and the reader recreating that same story through reading strategies, all construct an 'intricate web' of relationships; each act is linked to what Poulet indicates as 'a human intervention' that 'delivers [books and stories] from their materiality, from their immobility'.[9] Subsequently, the relationships of people in Etsuko's memory from the post-war period are fraught with meaning as she is mourning her dead daughter: how might the identities of these once-forgotten individuals intervene to help Etsuko recover a sense of a joyful, rather than stagnant, self?

Ishiguro moves one step beyond Poulet's 'experience of interiority' – or the way people cast their troubles in the dark regions of their minds – when he complicates or thwarts the revelation of his character's motives for remembering. In one scene, for instance, Etsuko remembers chasing after Mariko once or twice, and an episode she recounts at the end of the novel seems to be just another such event. However, as the conversation between the young girl and Etsuko evolves, the identity of the young girl becomes more confusing. Referred to only as 'the child' or 'the little girl', she could have been either Mariko or Keiko in this exchange:

'In any case,' I went on, 'if you don't like it over there, we can always come back.'
This time she looked up at me questioningly.
'Yes, I promise,' I said. 'If you don't like it over there, we'll come straight back. But we have to try it and see if we like it there. I'm sure we will.' (PVH 173)

The themes of broken promises and failed relationships haunt both her own and Sachiko's stories, and Etsuko's reconstruction of the stories tells us only that, while the outcomes of their lives were very similar, there remains much that will be unexplained. In leaving the identity of the child ambiguous in the above scene, Ishiguro emphasizes the pain of Etsuko's interior life; when Etsuko is able to turn the experience into a narrated event, the reader discovers that she is unable to derive any comfort from such overt confrontation with a painful past.

The various gaps and unavoidable silences produced by Etsuko's provocative memories are noted by Ishiguro, who declares that, more than a coherent account of one woman's past, *A Pale View of Hills* is the 'emotional story of how [Etsuko] came to leave Japan, although she doesn't tell you the actual facts' (GM 338). The author adds, 'But I'm not interested in the solid facts. The focus of the book is elsewhere, in the emotional upheaval.' While Ishiguro admits that Etsuko's memories are at times too 'clear' and too authoritative to pass off as those of someone suffering from delusions, he nevertheless wanted to cast his narrator as one who still had not resolved some important tensions about her life. In an interesting inversion of an observation that novels 'have beginnings, ends, and potentiality, even if the world has not',[10] Ishiguro shows how Etsuko's story must necessarily remain open-ended in order to produce its haunting effects upon readers. Ishiguro explains that Sachiko's character serves as a *doppelgänger* or spectral double[11] to Etsuko's as one way to show how people move through loss and death: 'Whatever the facts were about what happened to Sachiko and her daughter, they are of interest to Etsuko now because she can use them to talk about herself' (GM 337). Importantly, Ishiguro does not suggest that the relationship between Etsuko and Sachiko is an imaginary or supernatural one; rather, he expects the reader to be confused, though not daunted by the apparent similarities. Remembering Sachiko is one way that Etsuko tries to console herself about Keiko's death, and these memories are riddled with images of dying and death.[12]

While admitting to her own flawed memory, Etsuko also acknowledges the limitations presented by any singular point of view. In the same reflection, Etsuko observes that her second husband, a journalist named Sheringham who wrote articles about Japan following the American occupation, 'never understood the ways of our culture' (*PVH* 90). Her entire life with Sheringham remains untold, although the reader learns much more about her life with her first husband, Jiro, a seemingly traditional Japanese man. The untold parts of her life can only be inferred from the details she provides of the past and from her own revelations as she delves into that period. In this respect, even Etsuko's gaps are highly selective and call attention to her producing so many omissions in her tale.

Despite the many silent and unusual links between past and present that Etsuko subsequently creates, the reader is able to piece together a relatively coherent picture of Etsuko's life in the two periods. The reader engages in what theorist Wolfgang Iser identifies as 'a process of continual modification'[13] of Etsuko's story, in the same way that the narrator herself is apparently reading new significance in her evolving memories. For instance, Etsuko mentions twice in the narrative that, on the fifth and last morning of Niki's visit, she hears unusual and unexplained noises seeming to come from Keiko's old room; and, somewhat more frequently, she mentions that she has had recurrent dreams about a young girl on a swing, or, in other words, a young girl who is suspended by rope. Although she explains to Niki that the dream was inspired by having seen a young girl playing in a park while she and Niki were taking tea in town, she also hints that thoughts of Keiko's suicide by hanging has brought on the dream. In other scenes of the novel, child murders are alluded to, and, in particular, Etsuko recalls Mariko's enigmatic descriptions of unidentified and ghostly appearing women.

'Ignorance, imagination, illusion, and truth,' writes theorist Tzvetan Todorov, 'here are at least three stages through which the search for knowledge passes before leading a character to a definitive construction.'[14] These stages also represent Etsuko's futile quest for new knowledge of herself and her daughter. Interestingly, the actual bombing is never once mentioned in the novel, although evidence of rebuilding and healing from that devastating event exists everywhere in the physical surroundings.[15] The event is pointedly ignored, and only when Etsuko and her father-in-law, Ogata-San, are taking their walks is the city shown divided between areas that were hit by the bomb and those that remain unscathed. At one point they walk through

33

the park commemorating the dead; like the memory of Keiko that hovers over Etsuko and Niki, reminders of those who perished sadly compel the living onward. People's psyches following the bombing and Japan's eventual surrender are also revealed in interactions, such as unspoken grudges and resentments, that they have with one another. Their attitudes towards society, family members, and friends may be discerned from their words, gestures, or habits with one another; or, to explain it along the terms used to describe Etsuko's consciousness, people allow imagination and illusion to hold off their grasp of the truth, which emerges inevitably despite such mental interventions.

From the revealing clues of people's regard towards each other – particularly their evasions of postwar hardships – the reader learns that social interactions were of the imposed and not selected kinds. Etsuko had lived with the Ogata family after the bombing that destroyed her own family. At one point, Etsuko worries that she was a 'mad girl' (*PVH* 58) in those days, and Ogata-san assures her that 'You were very shocked, which was only to be expected. We were all shocked, those of us who were left' (*PVH* 58). In the time Etsuko lives with the Ogata family, she becomes engaged to their son Jiro, whom she marries under the condition that her future father-in-law plant her favourite flowers, azaleas, in the gateway. Ogata-san humorously reminds her of the incident, which Etsuko appears to have forgotten. Here, Ishiguro has Etsuko retrieve a forgotten piece from her failed memory, and this notable moment allows the reader to construct 'the novel's underlying system of values and ideas'.[16] Etsuko's memory is not only deeply flawed by her own admission, but it is even selective in how it expresses those flaws.

The period of Etsuko's friendship with Sachiko coincides with a visit that Ogata-san pays to the young couple at their post-wartime concrete apartment, and her memories of this period are also constructed from those gaps that she hopes will conceal her feelings. Etsuko's exchanges with her father-in-law suggest an easy relationship between them. As his visit extends, Etsuko realizes that Ogata-san has a particular mission to fulfil while he is in the city, and he had been soliciting his son's aid all along. Ignoring his father's appeal, Etsuko links her husband's refusal to assist with problems in their marriage:

I can see now, with hindsight, how typical this was of the way Jiro faced any potentially awkward confrontation. Had he not, years later, faced another crisis in much the same manner, it may be that I would never have left Nagasaki. However, that is by the way. *(PVH 126)*

What that other crisis was remains untold, but Etsuko's present understanding of a past event fills a small gap in her eventual migration to Britain. Rather than outwardly criticize her first husband, Etsuko presents him in a situation involving his own father, and, in this respect, Etsuko reveals much more about the subtle interactions between her family members.

Etsuko's outward devotion to her marriage and her role as a Japanese wife contrasts with Sachiko's more outward and irresponsible attitude towards family. Although Etsuko's exile to England reveals a more rebellious nature than she lets on, that aspect of her character is not evident in the past that she recounts. Gregory Mason observes that Etsuko's reported actions in the 'ellipses' of the novel show that she is much more unconventional than she appears (GM 338). Niki's exchanges with Etsuko also prompt a reader's awareness of her eventual choices to leave Jiro, Japan, and her native life behind – all daring choices made by a seemingly conventional Japanese woman. Etsuko's memory of her friendship with Sachiko may be a reminder that she eventually adopted attitudes similar to Sachiko's; if she intended to criticize her friend for her choices, she does so as an indirect way of reviewing and perhaps criticizing her own actions. In effect, she is a reader of her own life who is interpreting its significance from the distance of time and space.

When Etsuko refers to a happy occasion, the reader understands how sad and empty her present life feels to her, for the happiness seems so spare. At the very end of the novel, Etsuko gives Niki a picture of the hills over the harbour in Nagasaki to pass along to her poetess friend. She tells her daughter that 'This morning I was remembering the time we went there once, on a day-trip' and 'Keiko was happy that day' *(PVH 182)*. Denying that there was anything remarkably 'special' about that day beyond the fact that 'We rode on the cable cars', Etsuko in fact reveals how much she longs for the simple pleasures of participating in the world outside her dreary apartment. She recalls in vivid detail 'a pale outline of hills visible against the clouds [and how the view] brought me a rare sense of relief from the emptiness of those long afternoons I spent in that apartment' (*PVH* 99).[17] Etsuko expresses the long waiting accompanying those post-wartime days when she describes the 'unmistakable air of transience there, as if we were all of us waiting for the day we could move to something better' (*PVH* 12).

The theme of waiting – like the theme of broken promises – is present in her friend Sachiko's oscillating thoughts and these equivocations remind Etsuko of the consequences of her own uncertainties at a later time. Her friend's high hopes for escape to America may foretell Etsuko's own eventual departure from Japan. Meanwhile, Etsuko reports carefully the ups and downs expressed by her friend in an effort to understand her own later transformation. Sachiko's revelation to Etsuko at the end of their time together in Nagasaki is not surprising so much as it is brutally revealing. She tells Etsuko, 'Do you think I imagine for one moment that I'm a good mother to [Mariko]?' (*PVH* 171). Sachiko's false optimism may be compared to Mrs Fujiwara's hopeful attitude. Both women lost practically everything in the war, and, while the former seeks a way out of devastated Japan, the latter works to maintain a humble business in the country. Mrs Fujiwara also reminds pregnant Etsuko to maintain a cheerful demeanour in the face of motherhood, words that must ring ironic and hollow to her now in the present with the loss of Keiko. All of the characters in their respective ways try to reinvent the facts of their lives in the face of dreary reality; in this way, they are all engaged with producing alternate selves, or better shadows of their desolate selves. Sachiko's admiration for the Americans may be in keeping with the attitude in vogue in Japan following the surrender; older generations of people, such as those represented by Mrs Fujiwara and to an extent Ogata-san, endured their bitter losses through sustained work and their self-dignity; younger people, represented by Etsuko and Jiro, faced the uncertainties of their future with reserved stoicism and an approximately hopeful outlook.[18]

A Pale View of Hills is a simple book on many levels, but the surface tranquillity or simplicity underscores a more tumultu-ous emotional quality. Both in the mastery of tone and his evocative style, Ishiguro expresses so well Etsuko's story of the fragility of human life set against 'a field of force of destructive torrents and explosions'.[19] Expressed in the elusive and muted language of memory and set against the silenced landscape of post-atomic warfare, Ishiguro's first novel depicts eloquently a truthful version of how people must reconstruct their lives in order to move through the destructive forces present to them; people are engaged in the difficult task of reinterpreting the significance of their life choices following one of their nation's most horrendous crises. Aware of the force of death upon the living, Etsuko appropriately splinters her thinking and feeling selves in the narrative to produce a tale that is simultaneously painful and cathartic.

Etsuko's narrative therefore emerges as a post-mortem examination of her relationship with her dead daughter; it also becomes an effort to find suitable terms for her own remaining existence. In an effort to understand how death overtook Keiko, Etsuko returns to her own past, which is filled with signs and premonitions of potential pain and loss; from this, she seeks self-integrity and forgiveness at a historical moment when such qualities of human strength were in short supply. Her efforts of contemplation and comprehension, along with the ways she locates acceptable patterns for organizing her experience, are brilliantly captured in Ishiguro's first novel. Despite the absence of hopeful solace in this text, the reader's 'task of reinterpretation'[20] of Etsuko's tale provides the necessary impetus towards empathy with her character.

4

Deflecting Truth in Memory: *An Artist of the Floating World*

> No one likes to recognize himself as a stranger in a mirror where what he sees is not his own double but someone whom he would have liked to have been.[1]

Ishiguro's second novel has ageing artist Masuji Ono speaking on four separate occasions over a period of nearly two years, from October 1948 to June 1950. According to the author, an advantage of using a

> diary narrative is that each entry can be written from a different emotional position. What [Ono] writes in October 1948 is actually written out of a different set of assumptions than the pieces that are written later on.... so we can actually watch his progress, and so that the language itself changes slightly.   (GM 334)

The shifts between entries are subtle and they suggest Ono's modification of his stories as he moves forward.

Within each of his entries, Ono narrates two main events linking his past and present: life as a struggling then prominent artist and life as the family patriarch overseeing a fragmented family. Ono's remembrances, like Etsuko's, detail pain and loss; Ono's story seems to fill in gaps and elusive meanings as the novel progresses, but what occurs instead of discovery is the narrator's own version of life made more palatable in the very act of telling it. Indeed, though he does not 'lie' about his past in any conventional sense, he is anxious that some details from that period do not emerge. Ono's strategy prefigures for the reader of his tale a moment that reader-response critics identify as a 'reflexive movement of reception that is prestructured by the very form of fiction'.[2] In other words, fiction as a closed system corresponds to Ono's story also as an enclosed tale that undergoes internal and private – not externalized and public – transformation.[3] Ono's 'deception' is linked to his falsified sincerity in locating some form of truth about his life; in this work of fiction, Ishiguro has created a character who is the embodiment of 'fictionalization', and who seems both profoundly aware and ignorant of his condition.

Utterances in fiction, such as the ones by Ono, produce the dynamic situation of the novel, even when – as in this novel – the plot of the novel is more in the narrator's head than expressed through many physical actions. Contrived utterances particularly indicate that sense-making is related to 'attitudinal responses [such as] sympathy, revulsion, amusement, fear, or disapproval', which can be manipulated in language by the narrator.[4] Ono's way of telling his tale stems directly from the care he takes to direct a listener's response to his cause of self-reprieve. At the same time he proclaims to be telling the truth, he calls attention to his own distortions; Ono's slips may be read as accidental, or as moments when his façade shows through. Literally, Ono leaves traces for the reader's detection of his insincerity, while he remains ambiguous about his own knowledge of those slips.[5]

In October 1948, Ono is living on a war-damaged estate once belonging to the great Akira Sugimura, and he begins by positioning himself within distance of his home and recalling a visit paid to him the prior month by his eldest daughter Setsuko and her son Ichiro. Inviting the reader to view a part of the once-impressive home from the vantage point of a wooden bridge named 'the Bridge of Hesitation', Ono begins with a detailed account of the home's purchase. An 'auction of prestige' had been held by the bitterly divided descendants of Sugimura, and Ono was named most worthy of owning the home. During this introduction, Ono calls attention to and then tones down his former social status, thereby equivocating about the past.

Early on, Ono scrupulously presents a self-portrait of a likeable old man. The most significant piece of historical information – Japan's surrender after the Second World War – remains for the most part in the background of Ono's narrative.

39

He appears as just an old man reflecting with satisfaction on his many accomplishments; as the novel progresses, however, subtle ironies emerge. Standing in sight of his home as he begins the narrative, Ono gives the false impression that he can stand outside his life and view it objectively. Already in this scene, Ono reveals that the one writing his story 'is his own first dupe, and at the very moment he fools other people he is also fooling himself'.[6] By calling too much attention to his efforts to be objective, Ono makes his intentions appear more dubious to the reader. Furthermore, in later twisting the story's perspective to his advantage, Ono seems to arrive at a renewed understanding in the falsified views he presents to his listener. Like Etsuko, Ono establishes himself as interpreter of his own past and becomes a kind of 'reader for whom fiction changes into illusion to such a powerful degree that it finally replaces reality'.[7] The relatively simple shift from truth to lie to another form of truth is richly expressed by Ishiguro.

In order to gain empathy, Ono tells his listener that his memory may falter; like one engaged in a pleasant conversation, Ono moves from anecdote to anecdote as present events inspire his memory. However, in the middle of recounting an anecdote, Ono would break off saying, 'But I am digressing. I was trying to recall here [instead] details of Setsuko's stay with us last month' (*AFW* 28). Or, Ono provides us with a picture of a person struggling to stay focused when he characterizes his condition: 'It is perhaps a sign of my advancing years that I have taken to wandering into rooms for no purpose' (*AFW* 40). At other times, after the recounting of a particularly revealing episode, Ono stops short and admits, 'Of course, this is all a matter of many years ago now and I cannot vouch that those were my exact words that morning' (*AFW* 69). Momentarily, Ono's self-deprecation creates sympathy in the listener and distracts from his lies.

However much Ono struggles to present as many sides to a story as possible, though, the reader should consider Ishiguro's observation that the language of his novels 'tends to be the sort that actually suppresses meaning and tries to hide away meaning rather than chase after something just beyond the reach of words' (V&H 136–7). Is Ono purposely covering up the significance of past events or trying hard to remember them in their wholeness? As a form of self-portraiture, Ono's diary may be analysed as a work of art. A useful metaphor is expressed by Ono when he remembers a work made by a fellow artist nicknamed 'The Tortoise'. Ono remarks on how honest the visage appears in capturing some of his less flattering characteristics. Suspecting that 'earnestness and timidity' may be shadows coyly hinting at a more desired quality, such as 'a kind of lofty intellectual air', Ono reasons: 'But then to be fair, I cannot recall any colleague who could paint a self-portrait with absolute honesty; however accurately one may fill in the surface details of one's mirror reflection, the personality represented rarely comes near the truth as others would see it' (*AFW* 67). Here, Ono reveals an important truth about how one sees oneself in contrast to how others may see that same self. The effect calls to mind the startling philosophical observation made at the beginning of this chapter: 'No one likes to recognize himself as a stranger in a mirror where what he sees is not his own double but someone whom he would have liked to have been.' Intent on preserving his reputation now that the war has tarnished it, Ono unwittingly reveals that he does not truly recognize himself as the person he is reconstructing. Whether he accepts the futility of conveying to others the same fictionalized self that he envisions, Ono warns the reader that his own accounts may be questionable and may not correspond to the way others saw his character. But what is Ono hiding behind these feeble efforts of concealment?

Ishiguro explains that Ono's consciousness stemmed from his interest in creating a character who is mapping his own 'mental landscape' and who, in that process, is able to show that he 'lacked a perspective to see beyond his own environment and to stand outside the actual values of his time' (GM 341). Indeed, Ono's own blindness to his faults may become obvious the more he speaks. Ishiguro's 'ironic distance' to his characters – a strategy of the author hinting at their flaws or limits as they themselves unknowingly reveal these through their own speech or action – allows them to salvage dignity, a quality important to the author's vision of how people accept and deal with failure in their lives.

In episodes concerning his career as both struggling artist and respected teacher, or *sensei*, Ono slips here and there to indicate

41

how he was unable to explain his own values of independent thinking and judicious decision-making. Many of the decisions that Ono did make were the wrong ones or had devastating consequences; aware of these facts, Ono tries hard to cover up their implications for his own failed life.

Ishiguro explains that, in *An Artist of the Floating World*, he wanted to construct a character who was really no longer a part of the present world in which he found himself. Ono had made his decisions to support national imperialism when it was already gaining ground and reveals that he is blind to the way the younger generation now regards him. In describing Ono's 'parochial perspective', Ishiguro says that this novel 'is an exploration of somebody trying to come to terms with the fact that he has somehow misused his talents unknowingly, simply because he didn't have any extraordinary power of insight into the world he lived in' (GM 339). But, rather than pass judgement on Ono, Ishiguro acknowledges that people's very limitations are at times determined by their historical situations and the fact that they cannot know what the future will bring.

How can a person be certain that the decisions he or she makes at any point in life will yield a favourable outcome, as opposed to a detrimental one? This question forms the basis of an important exploration of self in Ishiguro's novel, since it raises the additional question of what a person should do after he or she realizes that mistakes were made. Reader-response critic Wolfgang Iser reminds us, 'Communication in literature is a process set in motion and regulated, not by a given code, but by a mutually restrictive and magnifying interaction between the explicit and the implicit, between revelation and conceal-ment.'[8] Reading Ono's story hinges on these polarizing ethical forces, which ask a reader to sort out Ono's sense of responsibility to his past. A similar concern will haunt Stevens in Ishiguro's third novel.[9]

Besides manifesting a self-flattering representation of his life as a famed artist, Ono is placating his two daughters as the younger one is on the verge of cementing her marriage negotiations. Setsuko's two visits in the novel's time coincides with her sister Noriko's transformation from an embittered old maid to a respectably married and then pregnant woman. Ono's account of his eldest daughter's visits prompts the reader to pay close attention to interactions among the family members – but only as Ono describes them. Besides noting the trivial affairs of daily life, Ono says every now and then that 'I got a distinct impression [Setsuko and Noriko] had at some point been discussing certain things about me' (*AFW* 83). He reinforces his own paranoia when he observes their quick glances at one another whenever he makes some reference to his past, to connection with some pupil from that time, or to reflections about his life. Ono's sense of his daughters' signs of discomfort about their father belies his own assessments of self-worth, and, as they grow seemingly more disconcerted with his view about the past, he delves deeper into that past to reassure himself and the reader that his daughters are exaggerating their embarrassment about him.

Ono's version of his professional life emerges in the context of his private, or family, life. The self-justifications evident throughout the novel seem to occur under the guise of protecting his family's name and reputation, but, as Ono retraces the steps of his past, the reader understands that pride more properly inspires Ono's constructed views. For, while Ono undertakes 'precautions' advised by his eldest daughter to protect Noriko's negotiations from falling through, he does so in order to remember the person he felt he was and had become. This person, he comes to realize in private but fails to accept in public, no longer fits in with the current state of affairs, and, in this regard, Ono is resurrecting his former self as a process of self-bereavement, as a way of mourning that lost self.

True to the way people investigate the meaning of their lives during a crucial transitional period, Ono looks back to his life as an artist in non-chronological fashion. He does this in order to piece together what he deems as a sufficiently full picture of circumstances for his listener. Aware that anyone living in his district would have known of certain trends before and after the war, Ono augments his listener's own understanding of the place and time and sways them towards his version of matters. Ono's interpretations invariably place him at the centre of the activity, even though he firmly adds that he did whatever circumstances required, as is revealed by the story about his role in the emergence of the nightlife place in the pleasure district called the Migi-Hidari:

I believe I have already mentioned the fact that I played a small part in the Migi-Hidari's coming into existence. Of course, not being a man of wealth, there was little I could do financially. But by that time my reputation in this city had grown to a certain extent; as I recall, I was not yet serving on the arts committee of the State Department, but I had many personal links there and was already being consulted frequently on matters of policy. So then, my petition to the authorities on [Migi-Hidari's owner] Yamagata's behalf was not without weight. (*AFW* 63)

The old pleasure district, which is on the verge of being sold as Ono concludes his narrative, remains the last place Ono is able to find reprieve.

Everyday life for Ono is fraught with tension, especially in his relations with those of the younger generation who believe the older ones advocated wrong ideals leading the nation to war and defeat. Ono's own stance is reiterated in his opposition to their view, and, in the scene where Ono's former student, Shintaro, is seeking to dissociate himself from his teacher, Ono angrily asks him, 'Why don't you simply face up to the past?' (*AFW* 103). Later, after Noriko's *maia*[10] takes a favourable turn, Ono reasons about that exchange: 'Shintaro would in my view be a happier man today if he had the courage and honesty to accept what he did in the past' (*AFW* 125). Ono's position is that Shintaro's cowardice is shameful, and yet, even as he disapproves of his former student's attitude, Ono shows that his own acceptance of the past depends on his creative manipulation of the facts. Indeed, what might constitute 'owning up to one's past'? This question is also at the heart of *An Artist of the Floating World*, and the very title suggests that Ono is suspended between two states, one that denies causing shame to Japan and one that responds to the effects of misguided principles. Those among the latter often committed suicide or *seppuku*, and in one scene Ono has an awkward exchange with Noriko's former fiancé about his company's President, who has just committed suicide as a way of salvaging honour. While the young man, Miyake, praises this action as 'an apology on behalf of us all to the families of those killed in the war' (*AFW* 55), Ono denounces it as a waste and a pity.

Even though Ono's daughters do not speak out against their father's view of matters, their actions and his suspicion of their meaning reveal that they too share the young men's view of a generational split in terms of responsibility for the war. Both Setsuko and Noriko express disagreement with him on trivial matters, such as those relating to Setsuko's son Ichiro or their father's ability to take care of the family house, as a way of dissociating from his ideas or ideals. Noriko is shown often as being moody or temperamental, and, while her angst is no doubt related to fears that she may never marry, her deep resentment against her father is evident in almost every scene she has with him. Importantly, the reader does well to remember that Ono can remark only on his interactions with her, and so what her relations with her sister or others are like are either not mentioned or only speculated upon by Ono. The gaps in the narrative, then, may be read as Ono's blindness to other people's dimensions at a time when he is so desperate to salvage his own dignity.

People's refusal to dwell openly on the wounds of the past, coupled with their veiled anger and resentment, characterize much of the human sentiment here. Bruce King observes that Ishiguro's 'characters avoid shaming each other by denying that anything of a critical nature is intended'.[11] If Ono expresses his disdain of or insensitivity to the younger generation's view of post-war life, he also reveals, at the same time, his alliance with them in maintaining silence or awkwardly feigned ignorance about the past. Indeed, Ono enacts in his narrative this provocative condition described by philosopher and literature critic George Steiner:'What is seen can be transposed into words; what is felt may occur at some level anterior to language or outside it.'[12] The negative attitudes swelling between people in the novel are often disguised, as Setsuko shows in her coy refusals to understand her father's meaning. Surface descriptions cannot truly underscore what is felt; indeed, what is really felt may be 'anterior to language' or inaccessible to the conscience and consciousness of the one speaking. This form of repression or inability to confront a version of one's reality forms one basis for Ono's clever evasions; it also establishes a troubling aesthetic for Ono's tale, one that entails a moment of comprehension that 'is not a movement from the unknown to the known, from the strange to the familiar'.[13] Or, whichever self-portrait Ono constructs for his listener is bound to be a false one.

Ono's inability to articulate and gain comprehension of the depth of pain is best expressed in the scene he has with Mr Enchi, a young man who is now residing with one of Ono's former pupils, Kuroda, a promising artist who went against Ono's teachings and was imprisoned during the war. Once Enchi discovers Ono's identity, he dismisses the visitor on Kuroda's behalf by declaring angrily though indirectly against what Ono signifies, 'We all know now who the real traitors were. And many of them are still walking free' (*AFW* 114). As expected, Ono's reaction to the meeting is one of subdued shock, and, as he contemplates further, he tries to understand the young man's resentment in the context of his mission to clear the path for Noriko's engagement:

> Naturally, I did not allow the young man's words to upset me unduly, but in the light of Noriko's marriage negotiations, the possibility that Kuroda was as hostile to my memory as Enchi suggested was indeed a disturbing one. It was, in any case, my duty as a father to press on with the matter, unpleasant though it was. (*AFW* 114)

Only towards the end of the novel, during November 1949 or several months after that meeting with Enchi, does the reader learn of the calamity that occurred between Ono and Kuroda, precipitating the estrangement between them. As 'the official adviser to the Committee of Unpatriotic Activities' before the war, Ono had reported his student to the authorities, who had arrested and then beaten Kuroda and interrogated Kuroda's mother as well. Ono's direct responsibility for Kuroda's suffering explains in part the dreary scene Ono described earlier in the novel of having seen a broken and depressed Kuroda shortly after the war (*AFW* 77–8). Kuroda's word against Ono in the present could have negative consequences for Noriko, or so Ono himself seems to fear. Importantly, Ono shows no remorse for what happened to Kuroda, thinking in mundane fashion at the time he spotted his former student in the dilapidated neighbourhood only that 'He's not young any more' (*AFW* 78). The many allusions to his most gifted and most betrayed former student indicate Ono's constant thoughts about him. Also unspoken is Ono's jealousy that his own student has far surpassed him in his artistic career. Confronting him again under the guise of smoothing over the past for Noriko's sake represents another moment when Ono acts as if he is the wronged man.

In the third section of the book, dated November 1949, Ono reveals more of his hidden sentiments about his life as an artist. While the emotional shifts from the first two sections to the third are quite subtle, Ono's interpretation of events and people nevertheless illuminates more serious matters. The reader pieces together the history of Ono's relationship with his own *sensei*, Seiji Moriyama or Mori-san, as well as that with Chishu Matsuda of the Okada-Shingen Art Society, who helped Ono transform his political views. From the events that Ono remembers, the reader regards the various moments of concord and discord between these two important figures in Ono's life.

Ishiguro thoughtfully characterizes the teacher–pupil relationship as a rather paternal one. Teachers guide and nurture their charges, who in turn demonstrate unrelenting loyalty to their mentors. The most accomplished pupils will themselves become teachers and perpetuate the cycle. Failure to maintain the balance of the relationship results in emotional and professional estrangement, leaving the disloyal one bereft of artistic support. The teacher–pupil paradigm is a significant one that is linked to the narrative strategy used by Ishiguro to reveal Ono's deceptive tale. For Ono, 'the act of narration is a process of disclosure' that has compelling contrary effects 'not unlike the well-known paradox of the teacher, who, to the extent that he or she is successful in educating the young, thereby renders them independent of the need for education and hence less likely to accord their educator the authorization to teach'.[14] Similarly, Ono must lie in order to keep his lies intact; more sympathetically, he must pretend to lose authority to speak about the past in order to resume his validity to do so.

The first teacher–pupil episode Ono describes involves his own father's dissatisfaction with his emerging artistic inclinations. In a scene guided by indirect accusations, Father sets out to discourage young Ono from a career in painting but manages only to kindle his ambitions further. In a much later scene, Ono describes an event between him and Mori-san, which is identical to the one that occurred between him and his father. Asked by his teacher to produce the remaining two or three

47

offending paintings, Ono tells him, 'I regret, Sensei, that I will not be able to find the remaining paintings' (*AFW* 179); this politely stated refusal to submit to the will of a paternal figure is a repetition of Ono's earlier defiance against his father. Sixteen years after leaving Mori-san's tutelage, Ono describes the rise of his own career, culminating in being awarded the prestigious Shigeta Foundation Award in 1938, some years before the Second World War and in the midst of rising nationalist feeling.

Promoted by Matsuda and the Society, Ono led a renowned career as an artist of nationalistic themes who socialized with his own students at the Migi-Hidari district. Ten years later, between 1949 and 1950 – or the time of the book's events some years after the surrender and when Ono's artistic convictions are no longer popular – Ono and Matsuda are reunited twice, and at each meeting the two dwell on the roles they played in world history. The last meeting between the two old colleagues takes place a month before Matsuda's death and provides the most revealing glimpse into Ono's sense of responsibility for his artistic work. Confessing to one another the lack of perspective each had of the world, Matsuda notes that 'there's no need to blame ourselves unduly. . . . We at least acted on what we believed and did our utmost. It's just that in the end we turned out to be ordinary men. Ordinary men with no special gifts of insight' (*AFW* 200). Later, Ono reflects and concurs that, 'we have the satisfaction of knowing that whatever we did, we did at the time in the best of faith' (*AFW* 201–2). People's self-absorption and their 'predisposition to stand back and view [themselves] as mere players in a game' fits with Ono's recognition of himself in Matsuda's words.[15] Ono remembers, as a way of consoling himself, that, 'however one may come in later years to reassess one's achievements, it is always a consolation to know that one's life has contained a moment or two of real satisfaction such as I experienced that day up on that high mountain path' (*AFW* 204). Ishiguro suggests that the assertion of individuality ultimately causes the teacher–pupil estrangement, itself a necessary gesture for the development of artistic, societal, and political ideals. Those who remain in a strictly tutelage relationship never truly advance in essential ways, and, in this respect, discord may be important for the progression of community, society, and nation.

Ishiguro notes that he is not out to pass judgement on his characters and that he is rather 'interested in people who do have a certain amount of talent...a certain passion, a certain real urge, to do a little more than the average person. They've got this urge to contribute to something larger' (V&H 151–2). However, limited by their situations or beliefs at a particular time, people cannot envision what consequences their actions will have or in what direction fate will lead them. The novel provides much exploration into the way people come to know but not always accept the ways they have failed. Ono's awareness of the cycles of tutelage present in families and professions attests to his belief that people are neither isolated from their circumstances nor estranged from the people around them. In this way, Ono's understanding of himself and his world stems from an extremely social view of life that requires a series of well-constructed lies to keep it intact.

However, the deaths of Ono's son Kenji and wife Michiko at the beginning and shortly before the end of the war, respectively, do not form an obsessive focus of Ono's remembrances; their absence seems to suggest that what remains at present is what matters for social interaction and discourse. Their deaths are mentioned in passing, and only as other people are paying polite respects to Ono's losses (Matsuda hints that his and Ono's estrangement years before is the result of some episode relating to Michiko). Too much explicit grievance over their deaths may begin a process of self-blame and regret that may be more than Ono can bear – after all, he supported sending young men like his own son to fight for Japan, and he remains proud of the Sugimura house in which Michiko was located when the freak bombing killed her. While lack of attention to their deaths may seem odd, given Ono's seeming commitment to family, failure or refusal to say more about their absence is in accord with Ono's narrative strategy. In other words, Ono talks around their deaths by focusing his energy on his daughters' futures; his strategy of survival echoes Etsuko's, whose tale is shrouded by death and grief but never explicitly stated in such terms. All of Ono's activities in the present time of the novel seem related to procuring some comfort for his family; only when his thoughts return to his past as an artist are we allowed into other dimensions of his being.

Towards the end of the novel, Ono proudly tells Matsuda that both his daughters are expecting children in the next several months; his tone suggests pride at being a part of their ability to extend the family tree. The theme of bearing and begetting children had appeared in *A Pale View of Hills* and was also related to the theme of death of a family member; the theme appears again in *The Remains of the Day*, when Mrs Benn tells Stevens that her own daughter is with child, as she talks around her feelings of loss concerning Stevens. Growing children themselves often have important, if seemingly peripheral, roles in all of the novels. In *An Artist of the Floating World*, the child Ichiro represents the effects of the American occupation in Japan. He is shown enthusiastically marvelling at the fetishes of America culture, such as the cartoon character Popeye. He is also a strong proponent of American individualism and idealism when he announces to his family that he will someday become president of the company for which his father presently works. And, like the rest of his family, he talks around the crucial issues, as his disappointment over not tasting sake one night shows.

Ishiguro observes that Ono's story is about 'the need to follow leaders and the need to exercise power over subordinates, as a sort of motor by which society operates', and that the reader might 'look at this not as a Japanese phenomenon but as a human phenomenon' (GM 342). Denial of a painful version of one's past amounts to the kind of effacement that philosopher Walter Benjamin describes as an inherently dangerous one for evolving societies: for one 'to articulate the past historically does not mean to recognize it "the way it really was" ' and that 'for every image of the past that is not recognized by the present as one of its own concerns [the past] threatens to disappear irretrievably'.[16] Ono's erasure of the stains of his past leave indelible traces, however, and his story prompts the reader to realize that Ono's reconstruction of his (inglorious) past 'in order either to confess or to engage in self-analysis, or in order to expose oneself . . . to the gaze of all, is perhaps to seek to survive, but through a perpetual suicide'.[17] Precisely because he appears *vulnerable* to the reader at every turn of his narrative – he is a beleaguered father, a lonely widow, an artist with a wronged reputation, a grieving friend – and because his response to his destitute states cannot be predicted by his daughters, Ono also gains a reader's sympathy: how could any one of us have performed or behaved differently from him?

At the very end, however, a reader's better sensibility takes hold, and Ono's false sense of himself in the context of world history resonates too much with a sense of self-inflicted wounding; his warped views of the past ultimately cannot offer redemption when his life is woven from such a dense fabric of lies. Ironically, Ono seems to know it, but he knows better than to reveal this knowledge to anyone else.

5

Disclosure and 'Unconcealment': *The Remains of the Day*

> For I always say either too much or too little, which is a
> terrible thing for a man with a passion for truth like mine.[1]

In the best known and most discussed of his novels, Ishiguro
cleverly weaves together the personal and the political, the
historical and universal themes of humanity.[2] Like Etsuko and
Ono, Stevens the narrator takes the reader into his confidence
and promises a perspective of clear meditation. But, Stevens's
declared enlightenment is a false one and promises nothing in
the way of a spiritual consolation. Has Stevens mulled through
these events long before and frequently enough so that what
emerges now is not discovery so much as a private confession of
those events? If so, what act of forgiveness does Stevens seek now
in a world no longer inhabited by Hitler and influenced by the
well-intentioned but misguided political involvement of his Lord
Darlington? Adam Zachary Newton insightfully discusses how
Stevens produces 'the appearance of a world which emerges from
behind the one he discreetly and courteously escorts us through;
we see that world, mostly unbeknownst to him, through a sort of
discursive double exposure'.[3] Stevens produces something like
two distinct stories of his life: set in two time periods – the past
between the world wars and the present as he undertakes his
holiday – Stevens's narrative incorporates both his knowledge of
and his blindness to the events he recounts.

Themes of memory, temporal dislocation, and emotional
estrangement continue to haunt Ishiguro's work. Here, Stevens
is simultaneously as unreliable and as sympathetic a narrator as

52

either Etsuko or Ono. Their stories promised a mode of detection at work: they both set out to understand the forces of the past as they faced the end of their lives and they sought to assemble some puzzle for this self-comprehension. But they also end their stories with keen but unspoken acceptance that the understanding is now futile knowledge. Believing that it is now too late for him to pursue romantic love or familial life in any conventional sense, Stevens at the end of the novel returns from his holiday to Darlington Hall, now owned by an American named Farraday, even more committed to living out the remainder of his days as a devoted servant to his master. What, then, has his journey through the past taught him?

By Ishiguro's third novel, the strategy of using two levels of narrative voice in the form of one character can be discerned more vividly: an 'extradiegetic' narrator who is ' "above" or superior to the story he narrates' and a 'homodiegetic' narrator who is a part of, or within, the story he tells.[4] Like Etsuko and Ono, Stevens is both types and he plays each role to fuller advantage, which calls greater attention to his dual roles. He wants the tale he is now sharing to reveal that his participation derived from living a life of the highest moral and professional virtues, even though he has difficulty believing it. Like Etsuko and Ono who wanted their listeners to believe in their naïve participation in past affairs, Stevens also casts himself as both progenitor of a virtuous life and victim of inexplicable physical or historical circumstances; in this homodiegetic role, he hopes to cultivate a listener's sympathy. Like Ono, he comes to believe fully in his version of events; unlike Ono, Stevens eventually reveals that this mask is too great a burden to bear and he is seen near the end sobbing. As Kathleen Wall clearly demonstrates, Ishiguro has constructed 'two contradictory voices that we hear simultaneously'.[5]

The subdued tone at the end belies the great anguish enveloping Stevens, who lets on that his empty life may have been a terrible price to pay for youthful optimism and adult commitment. He also seems excruciatingly aware that the ideals structuring his life in the past no longer hold, but he cannot quite bring himself to take any measures to counteract the emptiness now before him. Falling short of a full confession, his diary-like entries also fail to provide any recognition of need for change. At best, the novel ends on a note of anxious regret, with a variety of intersecting effects: readers sense that they know both more and less than Stevens tells, for what he conveys both reveals and conceals more than he actually expresses. In order to appear 'above' the story, he must cover up his tracks once he has unveiled a truthful version; he 'un-conceals' as he is on the verge of disclosure. Kathleen Wall correctly notes that the novel both facilitates and frustrates the discovery of truth, and that the text 'not only refocuses the reader's attention on the narrator's mental processes, but deconstructs the notion of truth, and consequently questions both "reliable" and "unreliable" narration and the distinctions we make between them'.[6]

All the assessments made of and by Stevens are represented indirectly and ironically through the course of the novel – and seemingly not always with keen awareness by Stevens himself. Or, that is the effect he perhaps hopes to convey and certainly the one that Ishiguro manages through a variety of clever narrative strategies; already, this technique had been used successfully with Ono's story. Like the second novel, *The Remains of the Day* raises a question about character that is an ethical one: is Stevens a conspirator of the failures now present in his life, or has he been an innocent victim of the exaggerated ideals of his profession? Towards the end of the novel, Stevens comes close to disavowing any culpability with his master's politics and defends his own decisions in what he believes are his own terms:

> I carried out my duties to the best of my abilities, indeed to a standard which many may consider 'first rate'. It is hardly my fault if his lordship's life and work have turned out today to look, at best a sad waste – and it is quite illogical that I should feel any regret or shame on my own account. (*RD* 201)

Throughout his encounters with people in 1956, three years after Lord Darlington's lonely death, Stevens finds that he can no longer account for the devastating demise of Darlington's good name and estate. However, he appears to defend his lordship until the moment revealed above; he may claim not to 'feel any regret or shame', but those are the precise feelings that have now overcome Stevens as he narrates his life with Darlington between the wars. He is unable to account for his equivocation without revealing the nature of his own wasted existence. Meera

Tamaya's view that Stevens's 'tragic truth of his past [is] a truth inextricably bound up with the history of his country' may confer too much value on Stevens' past *per se*, but she is perceptive in the way that she describes Stevens's clever narrating of that past:

> The brilliance of Ishiguro's narrative strategy is such that, just as Lord Darlington has convinced Stevens of the importance and nobility of his diplomatic maneuvering, the intimate tone of the narrative beguiles the reader into a curious complicity with Stevens' point of view; this enables one to empathize with Stevens even as the butler is completely taken in by Lord Darlington.[7]

A similar strategy of revelation and concealment had characterized Ono's – and, to a degree, Etsuko's – story, but here, according to Wall and Tamaya, Stevens's method is somewhat more insidious because he positions himself as having directly influenced world history; but, when he discovers that the influence was profoundly negative, he casts himself in an extradiegetic mode, where he can extricate himself from responsibility.

Most of the time, Stevens speaks with authority and confidence about being a butler. Like Etsuko and Ono, who admit to a failing memory, Stevens also asserts that he is remembering only as well as he can, given the confusion of the historical times and his emotional regard for people and events. Like those narrators, the gaps and inconsistencies in memory sometimes appear genuine. However, as in the two earlier novels, the emphasis on uncertainty also serves to distort and confuse versions the narrator desired to remain unexposed. In other words, though Stevens insists that he acted with the best of his knowledge given the circumstances and times, his story also reveals that these limitations conceal important details too shameful to bring out into the open. Newton characterizes Stevens's duplicity by the way he is able to 'glide through his memories, alternately looking and looking away'.[8] Moreover, Stevens seems both to know and *not to know* how past experiences shaped his present life.

Closer examination of Stevens's way of telling further reveals the tremendous trepidation he has in confronting the past, so much so that he creates a foil for the holiday/journey that he will undertake. 'It seems increasingly likely that I really will undertake the expedition that has been preoccupying my imagination for some days' (*RD* 3) is the opening statement of the novel, and it reveals Stevens's reluctance to face the prospect of an expedition that appears as a simple motoring holiday, but that is also demanding in physical and emotional ways.

Once given the idea by his employer, Stevens determines that the trip, if taken in the westward direction leading to Mrs Benn's home, could be very beneficial for securing additional household help at Darlington Hall. Persuaded by Mrs Benn's unhappy situation at home and believing that her letter to him is a ruse for returning to her former post of twenty years past, Stevens begins the journey with something like cheerful determination. As the trip progresses and Stevens rereads Mrs Benn's letter in the light of his reflections of the past, he grows uncertain of his earlier interpretation. His initial enthusiasm for her desire to return to Darlington Hall now wanes and he admits that 'I am inclined to believe I may well have read more into certain of her lines than perhaps was wise' (*RD* 180). The effect of Stevens's reading is one of 'progressive decertainizing', a term used by reader-response critics to show what occurs when an obsessive idea begins to take a life of its own, and, rather than creating an effect of certainty, the idea grows less clear and valid.[9] The weakening of certitude may be nothing more than the way Stevens ascertains the meanings of past situations. Or, Stevens's ability to rationalize and interpret diminishes as his disclosures become more like surprising revelations, and he loses control over his understanding. While Susie O'Brien's article takes post-colonial politics to some extreme levels, she is correct in her assessment of Ishiguro's attempts to subvert 'the notion of benevolent paternalism' through clever metaphors employed by Stevens himself.[10] In other words, caught unhinged by his careful distortions, Stevens distracts his listeners by calling a contrasting event to balance his tale; appearing as a 'good father' of his own evolving version of the past, Stevens can rectify moments when he slips.

Early on, Stevens is fascinated by a reference Mrs Benn makes to an event thirty years ago concerning Stevens's father. She notes in her letter that, shortly after Mr Stevens senior had tripped on the lawn carrying a full tray, she inadvertently sees him 'walking back and forth in front of the summerhouse, looking down at the ground as though he hoped to find some precious jewel he had dropped there' (*RD* 50). Stevens himself believes that the memory cited in the letter remains 'with Miss Kenton as it has done with [him]' and continues to note that evening he too observed his father's 'air of preoccupation' (*RD* 50). Shortly following the episode of the disastrous fall, Stevens is forced to admit openly that his father is no longer physically and mentally capable of the tasks demanded of a great butler; he is forced to accept Miss Kenton's assessments of his father's decline, and the acceptance is as odious to him as admitting to his empty existence in the present.

The reference in the letter is also important on a symbolic level. Like his father who searches for something concrete in order to understand what precipitated his fall, Stevens's own present narration becomes an attempt to explain to himself the impact of past events. Hoping to find 'some precious jewel' he may have dropped is an effective metaphor for describing lost opportunity and the futility of its recovery. In reading Mrs Benn's letter and then relating early episodes of their professional life together, Stevens begins to reveal an unusual attachment to Miss Kenton/Mrs Benn that is not merely the residue of the unexpressed love between them. In other words, he begins to associate her impressions with his own, so that, when she writes, 'I have no idea how I shall usefully fill the remainder of my life...' and that the 'rest of my life stretches out as an emptiness before me' (*RD* 49), he could well be identifying a condition of his own existence. This prospect seems to bear itself out at the end of the novel when he realizes – or perhaps has felt all along – that he had misinterpreted her desires to return to Darlington Hall and that, indeed, she has found ways both to understand and to accept the somewhat unsatisfying terms of her own life. At one level, then, Stevens's present journey to the West Country may be read as an attempt to rectify failure to connect meaningfully with Miss Kenton, who seems now to tell him something about himself as she is describing her own life. Jonathan Culler observes that such self-rectifying occurs 'by subjecting language to a dislocation which fragments the ordinary signs of our world...and challenges the limits we set to the self as a device or order and allows us, painfully or joyfully, to accede to an expansion of self'.[11] If Stevens is both above and within the narration he describes, he is also limited to a particular set of experiences from which he can draw; by 'dislocating' the meaning of selected past events, he is able to discover – with great pain or joy – further possibilities of their meaning. How Stevens 'expands' himself – either by enlarging his awareness or by reasserting the validity of his narrow vision – becomes an interesting focus of his narration because the vision is also very contradictory. Ishiguro comments on his deliberate attempt to reveal Stevens's false expansion of self, and the author frames it in terms of Stevens's unknowing relationship to the metaphors he creates:

> When Stevens says that [the greatness of Britain paradoxically comes from 'the lack of obvious drama or spectacle that sets the beauty of our land apart'] he is also saying something about himself. He thinks beauty and greatness lie in being able to be this kind of cold, frozen, butler who isn't demonstrative and who hides emotions in much the way he's saying that the British landscape does with its surface clam: the ability to actually keep down turmoil and emotion. He thinks this is what gives both butlers and the British landscape beauty and dignity. And, of course, that viewpoint is the one that actually crumbles during the course of Stevens' journey. (V&H 141–2)

At another level of the narrative, then, Stevens's physical journey represents actual departure from the estate that has kept him focused and confined not only to his sense of duty, but also to a possible mental and emotional 'expansion of self'. Most people conduct daily business with attention to past, present, and future events, for these temporal dimensions connect one's sense of self through times of changes and development. However, Stevens's mental journey to the past and his anticipation of the immediate, more physical future show that Stevens may be suppressing the past with greater awareness than he lets on. If he had hoped to dissociate himself from past affairs, those repressed events now return with a vengeance to his consciousness. Even allowing for a failed memory, Stevens cannot quite conceal the fact that he continues to be torn by choices he made in the past. Yet, as Stevens moves closer to and appears surprised by revelation, he devalues such benefit of hindsight, dismissing the fact that when 'one begins to search one's past for such "turning points", one is apt to start seeing them everywhere' (RD 175).

Part confession, part discovery, and part disavowal about himself in the various contexts, Stevens's story manifests his ardent desire to explain matters from his uniquely estranged perspective. A majority of Stevens's narrative, therefore, emerges as *explanation* or interpretation; as the novel progresses, a more discernible tone emerges, and it becomes possible to read his story as a defence against ideals even he now considers outmoded and in error. He is attempting to rework the lies that founded his life, but his efforts grow more transparent and his failure to produce an acceptable version of matters catches up with him.

Stevens undertakes his 'expedition' only if he can explain it first in terms of service to his present employer and, secondly, as justification for a much-needed respite from work. Even before he begins the actual trip, Stevens mulls through other seemingly unrelated thoughts, such as contemplating the question, 'What is a great butler?' (*RD* 31). While these sometimes abstract musings appear as distractions from the main event of travel, they in fact are important textural components of Stevens's life story. As such, the tangential observations or half-recalled anecdotes serve as significant pieces of the complex puzzle that Stevens will present, but perhaps not fully assemble for us. Among Stevens's first efforts of explanation, the terms 'greatness', 'dignity', 'honour', and 'professionalism' are all carefully defined and thoughtfully illustrated. Each of the terms may be seen in his service at Darlington Hall during the period he defines as his 'best years of service' (*RD* 61). Importantly, he also defines each in relation to his father's, and not his own, experiences.

Stevens recalls three distinct anecdotes involving his father in explaining how one in possession of dignity might therefore achieve greatness as a butler. Following these illustrations, Stevens emphatically notes that dignity 'has to do crucially with a butler's ability not to abandon the professional being he inhabits' (*RD* 42). Furthermore, maintaining a professional self requires one to control display of emotions and not to be 'shaken out by external events, however surprising, alarming, or vexing' (*RD* 43). Indirectly, then, Stevens reveals his great admiration for his father's philosophy; or, he presents the situations in such a way as he defines carefully the terms by which he hopes to be viewed and judged.

As he tells us after recounting his important role in the spring conference of 1923 at Darlington Hall, he recalls that period with 'a large sense of triumph' (RD 110) because he felt that he knew he had acted as his father might have done under similar circumstances. Later, when he recalls the trying evening of serving Darlington while he was in private (and probably illegal) conference with three important political figures, Stevens remarks that, while he felt 'downcast' (from earlier news of Miss Kenton's engagement), he soon experienced 'a deep feeling of triumph' and felt certain that he had served that night 'in a manner even my father might have been proud of' (RD 227).

In Stevens's mind, then, it appears that his father extolled the greatest virtues of being a butler. Excellence of service entails maintaining the important illusion that Stevens believes exemplified his father's professionalism. At one point in his reminiscences about butlering, Stevens describes the importance of achieving 'that balance between attentiveness and the illusion of absence that is essential to good waiting' (RD 72). Remarkably, Stevens has managed a brilliant metaphor to describe both his impending story/journey and his relationship to his father. Since these two events are related in an emotional way for Stevens, the metaphor of 'good waiting' is particularly apt for understanding the subtle difference between what Stevens will reveal and what he will conceal through the illusion of revealing.

Despite Stevens's manifest admiration for his father and his particular empathy for Mrs Benn's description of Stevens senior in her letter, the elderly butler turns out to be a rather unlikeable man. By extension, then, Stevens's idolatry of his father explains the self-abnegation that comes to dominate the narrative. When Stevens, as head of the household help, must convey to his father that his duties will be diminished with the forthcoming conference, the conversation between the men is bereft of any real warmth or consideration. Stevens senior has been sitting up for a few hours awaiting the beginning of the working day, and Stevens notices the prison-like cell that his father inhabits (later, Miss Kenton makes a similar observation about Stevens's own quarters). The two treat each other like the manager or worker each is; each has devoted himself to a life of professional service and not to forging what we might consider family geniality. His father's lonely life and death seem to prognosticate for Stevens his own impending isolation; to refer once again to Susie O'Brien's notion of 'benevolent paternalism', it appears here that Stevens has truly managed to subvert his father's existence by imprinting the meaning of his own life upon that existence. The evening of the 1923 conference is remembered by Stevens as being marked by periods of 'pandemonium', by 'an extremely tense atmosphere', and by 'efficiency and professional calm' (RD 97–8). These oscillating moods cast by his staff of servants reflect the inner turmoil experienced by Stevens, who will not tear himself away from his duties while his father lies dying upstairs. When Miss Kenton eventually brings him the news of his father's demise, Stevens pleads for her understanding.

It is not clear that he is experiencing anything like grief or shock at the news, for he never mentions such emotions in his account. It is only when Stevens serves young Mr Cardinal and Lord Darlington on separate occasions that both mention his looking unwell or as if he has been crying (RD 105). Stevens's post-mortem admiration for his father therefore strikes us as having rather dubious motives. David Gurewich keenly observes in his review of the novel that 'Stevens is not merely contemplating the meaning for butlering, using his father as an example. He is grappling with ways to justify his life.'[12] What does the evolving understanding represent to Stevens? Lord Darlington was a Nazi collaborator who was disgraced after the Second World War. Stevens knows what interpretation history has placed on Lord Darlington's life, but he cannot bring himself to admit this truth. To dissociate himself from his triumphant service to his good master, Stevens would lose all protective illusion of the usefulness of his life.

Stevens's encounter with the batman near Mortimer's Pond forces him to confront social interpretation of Darlington's role in history and to admit to the reader what he knows and believes. Calling to mind a related episode that might explain his reply to the batman, Stevens refers to a moment under his employ with Farraday. When asked by Farraday's guest Mrs Wakefield if he had worked for Darlington, Stevens's reply is an unambiguous, 'I didn't, madam, no' (RD 123). When confronted by Farraday later, Stevens offers a somewhat clever, if embellished explanation about it not being 'customary in

England for an employee to discuss his past employers' (*RD* 125). Reacting as if guilty of telling a lie, Stevens manages to suppress his association with Darlington. Also, he reveals that he wants to guard the illusion of his own life as a butler and indicates that 'I have chosen to tell white lies in both instances as the simplest means of avoiding unpleasantness' (*RD* 125–6). Why does Stevens not defend the 'great moral stature' (*RD* 126) of Darlington if he so adamantly believes it?

Stevens's assertion that he is 'today nothing but proud and grateful to have been given such a privilege' (*RD* 126) as service to Darlington rings hollow as events progress and as his own narrative strategy fails to conceal his shame. The spring 1923 conference was an effort to follow up on the international conference of 1922 in Italy, which was organized as a means to discuss the terms of the Versailles treaty. Darlington's sympathies for the Germans following the suicide of his friend Herr Bremann were roused so that he organized a private gathering of important figures in an effort to influence proceedings at the next international conference. Later in the novel, Stevens reveals that key officers of the growing Nazi regime were present at Darlington Hall, including people like Sir Oswald Mosley, leader of the British Union of Fascists. Towards the end of the novel, young Mr Cardinal guesses correctly that Darlington is out directly to influence and probably to manipulate British foreign policy in favour of Nazism when his lordship secretly meets key British politicians. Stevens's portrait of Darlington remains a sympathetic one, because he cannot divorce his unquestioned loyalty to his lordship without undermining his own devotion to serving him all these years. In other words, Stevens cannot agree with the views of public history without in part disavowing the truth of his private history in that same period.[13] These genuine tensions between outward truth and inward interpretation occur throughout the novel and signal Stevens's growing failure to keep all lies intact.

Stevens's role as narrator is more perplexing than that of either Etsuko's or Ono's, whose composure remained fairly constant throughout their tales, despite overwhelming evidence against the adequacy of their life choices. Readers of those two novels sensed deep sadness in the former and regret in the latter. Although all three narrators continued to dwell rather comfortably in their falsified versions of the past, it is Stevens who finds it difficult to move forward into a future containing his eventual retirement and demise. Perhaps he finds his own efforts at 'unconcealment' less gratifying or more shameful than the others, and he is unable to effect any solace from his own feeble way of reasserting meaning into past affairs.

One revealing moment of Stevens's divided sense of self occurs shortly after he arrives at the Taylors' home in Moscombe, Near Tavistock, Devon. Unlike the previous sections of his 'diary', in which he always recounts first the progress of his physical journey and then moves to events of the past, Stevens begins 'Day Three–Evening' with an immediate discussion of Darlington's purported anti-semitism. From there, he remembers several incidents concerning Miss Kenton when they had both worked together for some ten years. Either these memories seem to have been provoked by the fury to defend Darlington (and by extension, himself), or they are meant to distract himself from the deep embarrassment of the evening spent with the Taylors and their neighbours. As the Taylors' friends arrive following news of a great gentleman landing in their midst, Stevens inhabits his role by reinforcing their image of him. Stevens neither lies to them nor contradicts their belief in his importance. Later in his room, following a heated discussion, Stevens reveals his own snobbish belief that the common man, or people like the Taylors and their friends, can only live in the shadow of great men.

Stevens maintains his naïvety in both professional and personal instances of his life to great ironic effect. His small laughs in moments of awkwardness reveal his inability to deal directly with embarrassment or confrontation. When he presses himself to make particularly intense scrutiny of a memory, he lapses from referring to himself as 'I' to 'one', as a way to dissociate his present self from his past self. In one particularly giddy but absurd moment, Stevens notes not 'I' but that 'one would be meeting Miss Kenton again before the day's end' (RD 211). Presumably, 'one' gives Stevens the authority to question and examine his life in a way that 'I' cannot.

In an instance of such a metanarrative examination of the process of his memories, Stevens remarks, 'Naturally, when one looks back to such instances today, they may indeed take the appearance of being crucial, precious moments in one's life; but of course, at the time, this was not the impression one had' (*RD* 179). Launching himself onto this 'unduly introspective' and 'rather morose' state of mind, however, Stevens makes a startling comment: 'There was surely nothing to indicate at the time that such evidently small incidents [as I seem to recall now] would render whole dreams forever irredeemable' (*RD* 179). Stevens had been calling to mind those very incidents that he now disavows as a way of helping to explain something that had eluded him. By now disclaiming the power of his present memory to restore or maintain some more nostalgic version of the past, Stevens manages a clever reconstruction of the very image of self that he has produced up to this point. The reason for this negation is clear, as we notice that Stevens's reconstruction of himself proves less flattering the more he talks.

What exactly are the 'whole dreams' to which he refers above? And why are they now 'forever irredeemable'? While there is some logic to Stevens's refusal to look for clues or turning points through retrospection, there is also a deep sense of loss pervasive in the way his own memories are now indicting him. At this moment, Stevens is at the threshold of admitting that his entire life lies before him as a tremendous waste.

Stevens's choices had been predominantly in favour of establishing his professional persona over his personal life. Early on in their relationship, Stevens had expressed admiration for Miss Kenton's promise as head housekeeper. Shortly before the 1923 conference, she enters his room with flowers to brighten his quarters, but his refusal of her kind act precipitates an argument between them. Roughly ten years later, Stevens calls upon Miss Kenton to fire two Jewish maids at Lord Darlington's bidding; refusing to demonstrate his allegiance to her that the act is morally wrong, he leaves her with the impression that service to Darlington is his only and most important aim. David Lodge writes that Stevens's entire 'life has been based on the suppression and evasion of the truth, about himself and about others'.[14] Lodge's sympathetic assessment of Stevens helps us consider *how* we might come to embrace such an unadmirable character.

Ishiguro's presentation of Stevens's consciousness requires an 'embedded narration' that also characterizes the first two novels.[15] Direct appeals to the reader/listener of their stories allow the narrators to produce focused, if limited, versions of their stories; the intense relationship formed between reader and narrator creates in both novels the splitting and conjoining of reading and writing selves described by Georges Poulet.[16] The added dimension of what Poulet calls 'a phenomenon by which mental objects rise up from the depths of consciousness into the light of recognition' allows readers to sympathize with the pain of the narrators' experiences, because the errors made by Stevens appear as reasonably human ones.[17] Stories for these narrators are an effort of consolation, not merely a radical attempt to revise the already inscribed past. What is embedded in the ostensible narration is a tale of shame, loss, and regret: too ashamed and bereaved to confront the painful aspects of their lives, each of Ishiguro's narrators retreats into a more comfortable perspective. However, in doing so, they also reveal the tremendous anguish surrounding their stories.

Or, to cast a moral judgement against Stevens is to be entangled in a philosophical dilemma of 'wrongly assert[ing] that there is some kind of equivalency between the narrative act and the transparency of a consciousness'.[18] *How* Stevens has told his tale is as revealing as *what* he has told, but a reader's verdict on his moral character necessarily remains elusive, primarily because Stevens's story is a human story about loss and fear of that loss. He has told it to elicit sympathy and understanding, and, despite the overwhelming evidence against his own misperceptions, Stevens emerges as a somewhat compassionate character. Like Ono who revealed himself as a fool cowering from the past, Stevens too manages to sustain a surprisingly sympathetic illusion of his innocence in the face of a deeply shameful existence. Unlike Ono, Stevens finds the shame too overbearing eventually, and he succumbs to the pressure by exposing his deep vulnerabilities.

Even in the subtle transformations between Etsuko, Ono, and Stevens, Ishiguro has shown a remarkable grasp of human emotions and the way each might manipulate consciousness in order to placate their pain of loss. *The Remains of the Day* demonstrates what care Ishiguro has taken to reveal how people simultaneously deceive and protect themselves in the language they use.[19]

6

Seizing Comprehension: *The Unconsoled*

> We can be, in ways almost unendurable to reason, strangers
> to those whom we would know best, by whom we would be
> best known and unmasked.[1]

Zygmunt Bauman describes contemporary nomads as those
who 'wander between *unconnected* places' as 'they move *through*
identities'.[2] This description fits the protagonist of Ishiguro's
fourth novel, who is seen wandering through various inexplicable situations and places, accumulating a variety of identities;
dislocated from the centre of professional, societal, and familial
circles, Ryder embodies the indeterminacy of identity depicted
by George Steiner's remark above. Unable to fathom his own
true identity or sense of self – a theme already familiar to
readers of Ishiguro's fiction – the enigmatic Ryder cannot effect
any meaningful connection to what readers might determine as
significant other people in his life. For instance, how can Ryder
appear to have no memory of a life he shared with a woman
who might have been his wife and borne him a son? Despite the
lack of a clear referential reality in Ishiguro's fourth novel, the
themes of confusion and ostracism represent only a slight shift
in his views about how people manage their self-delusions.

Whereas flashback and disoriented memory characterize the
first three works, this novel, according to the author, depicts the
character not of someone, like the other narrators, who is
obviously 'looking back and ordering his experience, but of
someone in the midst of chaos, being pulled in different
directions at once, and not realising why (MJ 23). Ishiguro said
that this novel required a 'more emotionally risky' strategy

because he wanted to place his characters among more 'abstract themes' (MJ 21, 20). For some critics who admired the spare and evocative stories of the early novels, *The Unconsoled* represents a bizarre and entangled tale whose allegorical value is more dubious and whose parables are no longer those related to identifiable place, situation, and history. For others, the novel provokes an excitement that rivals the earlier books. Vince Passaro has an eloquent explanation to account for the above views, and he offers insight into Ishiguro's evolving fiction:

> Ishiguro's earlier books were lovely, shapely, delicately emotional, and, in terms of their intelligence, quietly forceful. Many of those attributes appear within *The Unconsoled*, but on the whole it is not at all an easy book – readers will find it difficult, especially at first, to live in this world of drifting reality and constant inappropriateness.[3]

Passaro's implication that the book might grow more lucid as the reader engages with the novel is somewhat too hopeful; Ishiguro's insistence on how Ryder's disconnection from people and places is 'unendurable to reason' (Steiner) persists until the novel's very end, while its message may be quite poignant.

In contrast to the other characters' development in the early novels, Ryder seems to accept more unconsciously than any of the other characters the futility of comprehending his existence. At the end of the early work, Ishiguro's characters notably confront a void that resonates curiously with assent, rather than resignation, as the dreary substance of their memories might presuppose. As desperate characters, these self-narrators indirectly manage to seize some final instant of painful awareness as acknowledgement of what is forever elusive or impossible to attain; even if their accounts never aspire to true denouement, they are able to delude themselves into believing they had achieved enlightenment. Ryder is similarly self-deluded, but his method for arriving at such a state is somewhat more complex than those characters of the earlier novels, and Ishiguro grants his fourth narrator a more unusual way of processing the forces of his life. If Ishiguro focuses on what he terms the languages of self-deception and self-protection to great poignant effect in the earlier work, here he is more interested in the unfamiliar world evoked by what the author calls 'the language of dreams' (DOK 148).

As such, Ryder is also a more difficult character to accept on the surface of things; while he seems completely unaware of his circumstances in the city where he is to present an important and major performance, he also seems to exert a powerful – if at times indirect – influence on everything that occurs in the novel. Conversely, the novel is riddled with scenes in which Ryder is completely ignored and deemed insignificant by the very citizens who seem to honour him in more public contexts. However, since Ryder is the one narrating events, it is possible to assess his reliability only in terms of what he seems to know as events present themselves to him. In other words, he seems to be more homodiegetic – or within, participating in the tale – than extradiegetic – or outside and above knowledge of the tale he is purporting to tell. This contrast to a narrator like Stevens in *The Remains of the Day* marks Ishiguro's shift away from a recognizable narrative strategy. Coupled with the author's emphasis on the unstable veracity of dreams, this novel emerges more precisely as what Ishiguro terms 'a landscape of imagination' (DOK 148).

The gaps of the narrative produced by the dreamlike forces of the imagination may actually reflect and explain the incoherent version of events provided by Ryder, who seems simultaneously at the centre and the periphery of what occurs in the novel. Rather than order the chaos that surrounds him in both the past and the present, or make an effort to seek whole answers, as Etsuko, Ono, and Stevens had set as their objectives, Ryder simply allows himself to become swept away by events. Throughout, Ryder seems both within and without his element; indeed, he seems thrust in a perplexing postmodern condition of establishing 'commerce with [the] unknowable', a condition that may be characterized best as Ryder's struggle both to seize and to avert comprehension of his life.[4] For Ryder, the world escapes explanation, and there is no practical point in grasping an evasive reality. If Etsuko, Ono, and Stevens are persuaded by a deconstruction of their pasts in order to gain a bit of self-satisfaction about their misguided choices in life, Ryder seems oblivious to such reasons for assembling and seems satisfied to dwell in a perpetually mysterious state. Therefore, if Ishiguro painstakingly, but delicately, allows his earlier characters to atone for their ill-conceived ideals, he thrusts Ryder amidst a murkier life; Ryder's existence is grounded in a profound insistence that reason is fallible, speculation unnecessary, and chronological unfolding with clearly established causes and effects a laughable premiss.

'Knowledge, conjecture, belief, memory,' writes Shlomith Rimmon-Kenan in his discussion of narration fiction, 'these are some of the terms of cognition'.[5] The degrees of a character's perception at each of these levels help readers reconstruct that character's sense of self, or *to know* him or herself within specific parameters. While these elements of cognition are present in more familiar ways in the earlier work, *The Unconsoled* delves into each of those realms of self-knowledge with greater irony. With each successive work, Ishiguro notes that he was trying to capture the complexities of the characters' emotional lives, or the ways each comes to terms with a life in which he or she had made serious mistakes or blunders. He also wants this book to be not ostensibly about either Japan or Britain. Readers who follow the ironic disclosures expressed by the early narrators are frequently troubled by the seemingly sporadic and uncontrolled leaps present in the fourth novel.

Even though comic situations occur in the early novels, they seem to fit the situation and context in more plot-related ways than in *The Unconsoled*, where comedy aspires to abstract and philosophical levels; critics became suspicious of the leaps in tone and with events that seemed too fragmented to make any sense. Despite what appears as radical shifts in the subject, mood, and strategy of the fourth novel, Ishiguro remains faithful to his task of presenting characters who are caught in circumstances beyond their immediate control but through which they then begin the arduous process of reconsidering and understanding their complicated lives. In other words, the complexity of the fourth novel is in proportion to the deepening of crises that affect contemporary people whose status grows more nomadic the greater their duties and obligations to matters other than the self. Ryder's efforts also appear more elusive than those of the early narrators, because, ironically, his problems are more ordinary than theirs. He lacks a political crisis more serious than healing from the effects of the nuclear bomb or from the wounds of fascism. Ryder's conflicts also seem to lack transcendence of meaning, which makes the narrator's purpose more puzzling: how can contemporary readers celebrate the ordinary and usual? The quotidian spirit of Ryder's problems lies at the heart of Ishiguro's evolving style: method of discourse, not description of situation, becomes the important metaphor for understanding myriad existence. In other words, not *what* Ryder struggles against, but rather, *how* he goes about it will reveal the meaning of Ryder's character and the implications of that character.

In terms of development, Ryder's seemingly capricious manner throughout the book is revealed in the end to be the mask concealing a tortured past wrought with loss, abandonment, and genuine feelings of worthlessness. Unlike novels that explore a character's wanderings and reveal a satisfying disclosure about his or her behaviour in the end, *The Unconsoled* does not deliver such familiar, desired, and expected outcomes. Rather, the reader is left as potentially confused and estranged as Ryder himself at the novel's end; it is a condition guaranteed to produce dissatisfaction and lack of resolution. In establishing an important, if uneasy, relationship with the reader, Ishiguro's work reminds us that, 'despite all potential references to reality, a fictional text is characterized by being a nonreferential composition'.[6]

Therefore, careful rereading of the novel's extensive dialogues between characters and efforts to cement disjointed narrative moments may initially fail to offer explicit and cogent explanations for the dynamics between people and their sense of both civic and personal responsibilities. In part, the fragmented nature of the novel contributes to the disconnections Ryder seems to have wrought upon his own life. A reader's dissatisfaction with the novel's outcome therefore coincides with disenchantment pervasive in Ryder's own situations. Whether this analogy of textual theme to readerly expectation 'explains' the novel's difficulty or emptiness is the issue raised by early readers of Ishiguro's 'new novel'.

Indeed, reviewers initially had a difficult time placing this fiction among Ishiguro's *œuvre* and seem at a loss to explain his bold, even audacious, attempts to reassess a narrative strategy that had proved so successful in capturing the complex emotional lives of his characters. Some of these critical views are worth a second look, since the language used to describe

Ishiguro's work bears relevance to Ryder's estranged self. A generous reviewer praises the book as one that 'is surely a metaphor for political crisis and personal disconnection';[7] a cautious reviewer calls it a 'discordant, plot-entangled, sometimes farcical nightmare of a book, that nevertheless offers worthy, if ponderous, ideas;[8] an irritated critic notes that the novel 'invents its own category of badness' and was for him 'empty, generally unaffecting'.[9] Another offers a thoughtful assessment of Ishiguro's 'emotionally risky' strategy and suggests that 'everything [Ryder] does leaves the lives he touches more miserable than before', and, in this respect, he

> resembles the protagonists of Ishiguro's three previous novels [because] he is completely unaware of the effects of his words and his behaviour, which are, ironically, entirely opposite to what he says and intends. He is, like those earlier protagonists, emotionally crippled and unable to act spontaneously or to achieve intimacy with others.[10]

From the very beginning, *The Unconsoled* takes considerable risk in maintaining a reader's interest.[11] Starting with an innocent enough scene – that of Ryder's arrival at a luxury hotel – the novel takes several peculiar leaps shortly thereafter. From porter Gustav's intense rambling about his fellow labourers' role in recent society to Ryder's inability to find a moment's rest from intruding presences, Part One of the novel attempts to chronicle the realistically impossible opening day of Ryder's arrival in a city that initially appeared as one foreign to him. Not only do the city's less illustrious inhabitants seem easily to distract Ryder's attention, but they also reveal themselves to be important caricatures inhabiting Ryder's own past and present lives. Thus, links between Ryder and the city's civilians are presumed to be much deeper and more sinister than one might initially presume. In effect, disinterested readers may abandon the absurd links, while others may regard with considerable investment the allegorical value Ishiguro attributes to his characters' roles. Possibly, Ishiguro is setting up a tale that resembles more a mystery than an account of memory directed at healing. The modes of detection and revelation found in the earlier novels have as an additional element in the fourth a darker and more inexplicable function.

Ryder himself is haunted by his past as he arrives at – or returns to – a city that holds the key to his success as a renowned pianist.[12] After brushing off the loquacious porter (who is soon to be revealed as Ryder's father-in-law), Ryder settles into his hotel room, only to make this startling discovery:

> I went on scrutinising the ceiling for some time, then sat up on the bed and looked around, the sense of recognition growing stronger by the second. The room I was now in, I realised, was the very room that had served as my bedroom during the two years my parents and I lived at my aunt's house on the borders of England and Wales. (*U* 16)

After noticing that some changes had been made to the present room, Ryder remembers a childhood event that occurred in this room and that subsequently became 'a key factor in many of the battles I subsequently orchestrated' (*U* 17). The memories of childhood and the familiarity of home instil in Ryder a false but 'profound feeling of peace' (*U* 17) and he is able to drift off to rest. However, the repetition of similar scenes of interruption will continue to haunt Ryder's stay. Though initially absurd, the above scene shows how Ishiguro mixes psychology with the character's sense of material reality to produce a compelling scene in which past and present merge.

Were the scene not so strange, it would be sensible to dismiss it as a sign of Ryder's homesickness or the distress of travel itself. However, in later scenes, Ryder is called to remember the connections of his present visit with significant people or moments related to his past. A particularly absurd connection is made when Ryder sees the remnants of his family's ancient car on an open field near the building where he is to make his major performance. Looking at the old wreck, Ryder is stunned that 'I was looking at the remains of the old family car my father had driven for many years' and how 'in this sad state [it] had brought back to me its final days with us, when it had become so old I was acutely embarrassed my parents should continue to go about in it' (*U* 261). Everywhere in the novel, Ryder bumps against people, places, and objects recognizable to him from an obscure past. Such familiar objects cast in intentionally absurd situations or conditions further strengthen Ishiguro's view that one's dreams and imagination have great potency.

Later, the odd connection Ryder makes between himself and the porter's daughter and grandson, Sophie and Boris, is a particularly distressing one, since Ryder initially feigns complete ignorance of them. As their encounters multiply, the reader learns from Ryder himself that not only does he have a deep and extended relationship with them; he may in fact have abandoned them in pursuit of his musical career. His amnesiac condition makes us wonder what he may be concealing. How can Ryder appear not to know the apparent mother of his child, the son he seems to have fathered, and the nature of their separation? Why does he make half-hearted gestures towards a reconciliation, when he has no idea what their lives are (now) like? Sophie's final remarks to Ryder at the novel's end offer an unfulfilling closure to their relationship: 'Leave us. You were always on the outside of our love. Now look at you. On the outside of our grief too. Leave us. Go away' (U 532). And yet Sophie's admonishment is the appropriate one, for Ryder remains as oblivious of them at the end as he was at the beginning of the novel. Indeed, she notes for us that Ryder's peripheral status in their lives may mirror other aspects of his existence.

Wandering in the strange, yet strangely familiar, city, Ryder meets familiar people such as Geoffrey Saunders, 'who had been in my year at school in England' (U 44), and Fiona Roberts, an old friend 'from my village primary school in Worcestershire with whom I had developed a special friendship around the time I was nine years old' (U 171). Their efforts to welcome the renowned pianist to the town are met with Ryder's bizarre resistance, as they make special efforts to meet him. Everywhere Ryder turns, people approach him and ask for something from him, whether to have tea or a meal, or to make an important statement that might help them work through their community crisis. Although he promises to meet their requests, he more often than not fails to do so or fully to acknowledge them.

Perhaps more unusual than the pressing demands of 'old friends' is Ryder's ability to read the minds of other people and to assess their emotional lives in contexts obviously unknown to him. The first evidence of Ryder's clairvoyance appears when he accepts a ride from the hotel manager's son, Stephan Hoffman, who is himself an aspiring pianist. *En route* back to the hotel after a labyrinthine journey to Sophie's house with a tired Boris,

Ryder gladly accepts a ride from Stephan, who interrupts the trip with a visit to Miss Collins. The elderly matron of arts receives her visitor while Ryder waits in the car. Nevertheless, from the distance of an enclosed car, our protagonist is able to fathom not only the substantial script of their conversation but their intonations and cadences as well. Also, Ryder is able to conjure up Stephan's intimate thoughts as they drive through deserted city streets:

> The young man [Stephan] remained silent for a long time and I wondered if he had become angry with me. But then I caught sight of his profile in the changing light and realised he was turning over in his mind a particular incident from several years ago. It was an episode he had pondered many times before – often when lying awake at night or when driving alone – and now his fear that I would prove unable to help him had caused him once more to bring it to the front of his mind.
>
> It had been the occasion of his mother's birthday.   (*U* 65)

As events progress, it becomes apparent that Ryder's 'ability' to penetrate Stephan's thoughts is related to his own concerns about parental acceptance. Using Stephan's presumed past to access aspects of his own, Ryder's strategy for dealing with a painful past reminds us of the ways in which Ishiguro's other protagonists found ways to confront their lives: by remembering events of other people's lives, they begin to assess the meaning of their own. This approach both reflects and deflects their own pained pasts onto the present narrative.

The Unconsoled is punctuated with Ryder's remembrance of his parents' behaviour towards him and one other. Various episodes recalled by Ryder bear resemblance to events in which his presumed son Boris is the focus of attention. The strategy of remembering one's own painful past in the context of another person's was developed by Ishiguro in his previous novels. Etsuko's memory of a fleeting friendship with Sachiko in *A Pale View of Hills* is a foil for confronting her own tortured past; in *An Artist of the Floating World*, Ono's remembrance of his teacher, Mori-San, mirrors the way he as a teacher erroneously served his own pupils years later; and, in *The Remains of the Day*, Stevens remembers his own life as a kind of palimpsest of his father's. In *The Unconsoled*, Ishiguro turns the strategy of substituting another's past for one's own to comic, even bizarre, effect.

74

The greatest worry on Ryder's mind throughout the novel concerns his performance. He is agitated when he is unable to practise his programme, but what lurks (and remains unspoken) in his mind is hope that his parents arrive safely in the city and that they show up for his performance. Nevertheless, he fails to take any concrete measure to ensure that this sequence of events occurs. At the novel's end, Ryder strides into the offices of Miss Stratmann, the public-relations officer at the hotel, and demands to know his parents' itinerary. Miss Stratmann questions Ryder's presumptions until he remarks with embarrassment:

> 'Surely, it wasn't unreasonable of me to assume they would come this time? After all, I'm at the height of my powers now. How much longer am I supposed to go on travelling like this? Of course, I'm sorry if I've put anyone to unnecessary inconvenience, but surely it won't come to that. They must be here somewhere. Besides, I heard them. When I stopped the car in the woods, I could hear them coming, their horse and carriage. I heard them, they must be here, surely, it's not unreasonable . . . '
> I collapsed into a nearby chair and realised I had started to sob. (U 512)

Miss Stratmann's subsequent empathy fails to console Ryder, who reveals the unspoken hope throughout the novel that he had been waiting for his parents all along. Ryder's breakdown calls to mind Stevens's final disavowal at the end of that novel, and both cases of despair signal Ishiguro's staple emphasis on his characters' emotional conditions.

The irony of Ryder's hope is that it contrasts so vividly with his relationship with Boris. Indeed, Ryder's estrangement from Boris, despite his own calculated efforts to rejoin his 'son', runs counter to his own experiences. Hoping to produce a parent–child relationship different from his own neglected one, Ryder replicates his own wounds onto Boris. In one scene, Ryder noticeably ignores the young boy, even though Boris clearly seeks Ryder's attention. In response, Ryder notes offhandedly that, while he 'had the distinct impression [Boris] was trying to address me', he 'went on reading' without paying heed to the young boy (U 287). Sadly, Boris has just received the 'gift' of a handyman's manual from Ryder and Sophie, and he feigns deep interest in knowing how the book 'shows you how to do everything' (*U* 287). What the manual cannot show, of course, is how to unite this fragmented family, their shattered (if not shared) past.

Even as Ryder manages to commit to a social situation with his 'family', he is peculiarly critical of Sophie's ability to make the evening a successful one:

> Moreover, it was not even as though she had particularly excelled herself with the cooking. She had not thought to provide, for instance, any sardines on little triangles of toast, or any cheese and sausage kebabs. She had not made an omelette of any sort. (*U* 288)

Ryder's list of defects on Sophie's hostess role is somewhat hilarious, until we realize that the absurdity of his charge stems as well from other arenas of unfulfilment in his life.

Notably, Ryder seems unaware of the way people around him respond to him as a human being. On the surface, he is simply a famous pianist who has landed in their town for a performance. In effect, he symbolizes the possibility of a resolution for them, although he remains unaware of the agenda for such a social reform. One absurdly humorous episode involves posing in front of the Sattler monument on a photo shoot with a local journalist. While the journalist and his photographer, Pedro, construct the photograph, they mock Ryder in loud tones. Ryder seems not to have registered the insults they throw his way and seems more conscious of their false praises of him. And yet he records their conversations in his narrative *as if* he understood what they were saying. Ryder's response to the situation may reflect that of the readers of this novel: not understanding in the least what something means, one can still manifest action *as if* one did in order to save face.

Other incongruous events riddle the narrative. When Ryder and Boris board the bus to the lake, they encounter a fellow passenger who manages to assemble an entire scene prefiguring their arrival. The man speaks as if he has intimate knowledge of objects, places, and events significant to Ryder and Boris. In this way, he prognosticates entire sequences of events for the two. Similarly, Ryder continues to see events in their presumed entirety, when, in actuality, physical circumstances preclude him from doing so. A poignant event occurs when Ryder is able to see Stephan Hoffman perform for his parents on the important night in question. Not only is he said to have a grand view of the scene from a lofty position in the performance hall (which he could not, given the physical descriptions); he is also able to see the responses meted by Mr and Mrs Hoffman, as well as Stephan's own emotional response to his programme (which he cannot, if he is physically located in the space he describes). In these ways of manipulating his reality by altering a physics of space, however, Ryder imagines, or hopes to have materialize before him, the reception of his own parents for his performance.

Unfortunately, fulfilment is not a part of this novel's agenda, and Ryder's thwarted expectations serve as an important motif for the novel, which Ishiguro himself notes is about 'performance anxiety'.[13] In examining the theme of how people *act* in public contexts, we might remember a postmodern assessment that 'there are accretions of everyday life which are still – in ... cultural practices – felt as impediments to performance', so that all rehearsals towards a final act become just that, simply preparations – and not significant moments of closure – for that calculated moment.[14] As a performer, Ryder acts in accordance with what others wish from him: Gustav's plea that Ryder talk to his daughter Sophie and grandson Boris *and* attend a meeting of porters; hotel manager Hoffman senior's request that he peruse his wife's scrapbooks of Ryder's performances; Stephan Hoffman's favour of direction and guidance for his own piano recital; old classmates' hope for tea, a meal, or some other social gathering in which Ryder would be the honoured guest; important civic figures' expectation that Ryder will help them solve an important community crisis; and Sophie's desire for a reunion with Ryder in order to produce a family unit. Amidst these impossible obligations, Ryder intends to sort out the crisis involving the dethroned Christoff and the resurrected Brodsky, two local but otherwise insignificant celebrities, who had at one time represented the correct artistic values of the community. How long before readers guess that not only will Ryder fail at each endeavour, but that all along he has been involved in a fruitless chase? Not surprisingly, then, the promised piano performance by Ryder never materializes.

Inhabiting so many different realms and spatio-temporal dimensions, Ryder metaphorically performs the very dislocations experienced by people in the late twentieth century who understand intuitively that a meaning of life is 'indeterminate but it is "investigable" '.[15] The multiple choices possible in any given existence also perplex people like Ryder, who has now come to represent every contemporary person: how can we expect those closest to us to assist in this investigation when they are but strangers to us? Unable to forge genuine human ties with other people, Ryder wanders with aimless purpose in the novel, and his adventures compel readers to identify with the truth of contemporary existence: deep loneliness and isolation are at the heart of the flurry of social activity for us contemporary nomads. What comprehension we might seize of life's meaning is as fleeting and disconnected as it is unfulfilling.

Ishiguro finds himself defending the shifts that he undertakes in the fourth novel. Most often, his 'explanations' appear coherent and correspond to remarks of other reviewers who respect the author's shifts in tone, apparent subject, and novel direction. In one explanation of Ryder's incongruent character-ization, Ishiguro expresses his recurrent concern with writing novels that have an allegorical value to the way people conduct their lives:

> Often Ryder looks a bit odd because he promises a kid something and then turns around and forgets. Over the course of a lifetime, we do this the whole time. You promise friends that you'll always be friends, or spouses that you'll always be together; or that you're going to live a certain way, and then you meet that same person five or six years later and they're doing something completely different. You don't think that they are completely mad or amnesiac or something, but just that that's the way life is because five or six years have passed. It's only when you look at it from a certain perspective and compress it into a few days that it starts to look like very strange behavior. (DOK 153)

Ryder's lack of a more identifiably conscious awareness of his many situations subsequently reminds readers of the tenuous ways in which we locate fulfilment or understanding in conventional realist terms. Ryder's 'transcendence' is as impossible as those of Etsuko, Ono, and Stevens, because each has had his or her past distilled and compressed into a self-narrative evolving over only a few days. Unlike those other characters, however, Ryder produces a more curious post-modern condition of knowledge of the not-known, or more generally, [a] relation with the unknown . . . a relation that excludes, therefore, ecstatic confusion (that of fear), mystical participation, but also appropriation, every form of conquest, and even, when all is taken in to account, the seizing that comprehension always is.[16]

In other words, like the others who embarked on a knowledge of self and private history, Ryder by contrast reveals that life is not an open book to be read and interpreted; indeed, the disclosures are more often too painful or too elusive to confront and accept or alter. Living in a state of not-knowing may be unsettling, but the paradox of doing so may be closer to the 'truth' that Ishiguro expresses in his fiction as the governing principle of human lives.

While the fourth novel does not dismantle key and familiar ways in which we seek consolation in life, it does raise additional questions about the relationship people have to one another when they hope to locate catharsis in their lives. All of the early narrators had the dubious benefit of speaking about those who had already died, become disabled from speech, or otherwise disenfranchised from the main protagonist's life; Ryder's return to a presumably repressed past is much more confrontational, in that his encounters occur in the space of his present narration. The other narrators forge acceptable spatial, temporal, and physical distances between past and present. Startled, alarmed, and disoriented by his encounters, Ryder, by contrast, stumbles through a life with all the elements and resonances of a recognizable past, but not surprisingly, in dreamlike confusion, he eventually evades responsibility from them all, as the last scene on the tram demonstrates. In fiction, one can follow through with evasion; Ishiguro tells us that, in reality, actual people might not do the same and expect emotional consolation.

Close reading of all of Ishiguro's novels reveals his compassionate sense of human strengths and flaws, his deep awareness of how people come to represent the glorious and shameful aspects of their lives. He admires their courageous, but futile, attempt to face painful events. And he writes their stories with respect for how people console themselves through necessary emotional manipulation.

The mixed reception of *The Unconsoled* signals a shift in popular sentiment towards Ishiguro's work, but the intensity of both negative and positive critical views also reflects the author's commitment to evolving his art. Not content to be trapped into a style for which he had received abundant praise in the past, Ishiguro is encouraged by the richness of human existence to keep exploring new forms of aesthetic representation. Future novels should inspire eager readers, for better or worse.

The reader–writer paradigm explored in this study highlights Ishiguro's own role as a perpetual interpreter of the world. The surface eloquence of his works simultaneously masks and exposes the deeper emotional turmoil of his narrators. Each of Ishiguro's novels thus far expresses both the durability and the fragility of the human spirit, or what Etsuko observed as the nature of humans always to look onward to something better.

Postscript: Ishiguro's Work in Progress

Ishiguro is a relatively young novelist who has already garnered many major literary prizes, and readers can expect new or unusual work by the author in the new century. Already, a fifth novel was in press as I completed this study of his first novels, published in Great Britain in April 2000.

The protagonist of *When We Were Orphans* is Christopher Banks, a celebrated London detective in the 1930s who returns to his birthplace, Shanghai, in order to solve a mystery that has always eluded him: the kidnapping and disappearance of his parents when he was a child of ten. The people of Shanghai accept Banks's notion that resolution of the mystery will help avert major world catastrophe. With the Second World War looming, Banks believes that he can save civilization, prevent Japan from invading Shanghai, and find personal solace for himself in the process; his mission has vast implications, and the people of Shanghai welcome and assist him in the task.

Ishiguro says, 'The hero's actions are governed by a rather odd logic deriving from his childhood. His parents disappeared when he was ten, and in some strange way, he believes his parents are still being held captive and will be freed when he solves the case. The child's logic has been carried into the adult world' (CW2).

In describing the tone and structure of the novel, Ishiguro refers to some aspects which appeared in the earlier novels, but he adds, 'Obviously, I'm hoping that this novel does a few things differently' (CW2). *When We Were Orphans* is a medium-length novel of about 300 pages that is divided into two major parts, and it concludes with an epilogue depicting events in the 1950s, when the actual war is over and Banks has returned from

Shanghai to London.

Memory is a shaping, as well as a distorting, force in Banks's first-person account. Ishiguro indicates that the first part of the novel combines Banks's present life with his memory of an earlier period in Shanghai. Ishiguro describes Banks as being complacent in the first part of the novel, since he is a character who is experiencing a successful career. As Banks remembers life with his parents in Shanghai and the novel moves forward with his determination to uncover the truth of his parents' disappearance, the character becomes increasingly agitated, until internal pressure becomes so great that Banks must confront the way his entire world view is undergoing revision.

The first part is crucial for establishing the identities of Banks's parents, and his mother figures quite prominently in these memories of the adult Banks, providing an important thread to the novel's development. The reader learns from Banks's retrospective account that young Christopher was raised by his aunt in England following his parents' disappearance, and that he eventually comes to London as an adult. Ishiguro adds that the first part almost resembles a 'normal realist novel', certainly more so than his preceding novel, *The Unconsoled*. There is even a sub-plot which involves a love story concerning Banks.

The second part of the novel shows Banks in Shanghai, ostensibly solving the mystery. In effect, this part also establishes the durability of Banks's childhood emotions as these wended their way into his London detective life. Here, Ishiguro describes his intended technique. 'This is another take on memory. Some passages may have a vaguely Proustian quality, in that Banks is dealing with faint and murky images from his past as he tries to piece together the truth about what happened back then' (CW2).

While there are no 'out and out evil characters' in this novel, Ishiguro notes that there is a treacherous figure present, and that there are numerous obstacles to Banks's quest. In the end, though, Ishiguro says that the novel has a denouement and provides an explanation; readers do learn in some tangible fashion what happened to Banks's parents. As might be expected, a note of sadness punctuates the ending, since Banks must abandon his child's vision or memory.

Notes

INTRODUCTION

1. The most famous instance of this character, which could not have escaped Ishiguro, comes from P. G. Wodehouse (1881–1975). Wodehouse's butler, Jeeves, is a somewhat different character from Ishiguro's Stevens, since both authors obviously have different aims in their novels.
2. See Sybil Steinberg (in *Publisher's Weekly* (18 Sept. 1995), 105–6) for Ishiguro's reaction to the film.
3. *An Artist of the Floating World* was shortlisted for the Booker Prize in 1986, but it won the Whitbread Book of the Year Award instead.
4. Brian W. Shaffer (*Understanding Kazuo Ishiguro* (Durham, SC: University of South Carolina Press, 1998)), discusses some of the origins of these comparisons (p. 6).
5. Told to Steinberg, in *Publisher's Weekly*, 106.
6. The implications of children's roles in all of the novels are not very explicit, but they relate to a theme of hope and future: in Asian language, 'to give birth' is represented by the Chinese and Japanese ideograms that mean 'the next generation coming out'.
7. Steinberg, in *Publisher's Weekly*, 106.
8. Georg Lukács (*The Theory of the Novel*, trans. Anna Bostock (Cambridge, Mass.: MIT Press, 1971), 29), makes this statement from the philosopher Novalis's view about living and ways in which people represent that living.
9. His application for British citizenship in 1982 was 'relatively easy' (CW). With immigrant status alone, Ishiguro could not have qualified for most of Britain's major literary prizes.

CHAPTER 1.   ISHIGURO AS AN INTERNATIONAL WRITER

1. Salman Rushdie, 'Kazuo Ishiguro', in *Imaginary Homelands: Essays and Criticism, 1981–1991* (London: Viking, 1991), 244.

83

2. When he accepted his prize in 1989, Ishiguro poignantly said: 'It would be improper for us not to remember Salman Rushdie this evening and think about the alarming situation and plight in which he finds himself.'

3. Bruce King, 'The New Internationalism: Shiva Naipaul, Salman Rushdie, Buchi Emecheta, Timothy Mo and Kazuo Ishiguro', in James Acheson (ed.), *The British and Irish Novel since 1960* (New York: St Martin's Press, 1991), 193.

4. Salman Rushdie (' "Commonwealth Literature" Does Not Exist', in *Imaginary Homelands: Essays and Criticism, 1981–1991* (London: Viking, 1991), 61–70) offers an interesting perspective on the dilemma of labelling writers whose cultural origins are not Anglo. It is not far-fetched to read Etsuko's story in *A Pale View of Hills* from her perspective as an immigrant, but perhaps 'exile' is the more appropriate term here.

5. 'The New Internationalism', 193.

6. Edward Said, *Orientalism* (New York: Vintage Books, 1979).

7. King, 'The New Internationalism', 207.

8. See Pico Iyer's review, 'Waiting upon History', *Partisan Review*, 58 (1991), 585–90, for his remark that the novel is a 'perfectly English novel that could have been written only by a Japanese'. See also Francis King, 'A Stately Procession of One', *Spectator* (1989), 31–2, for a first-world attitude about Ishiguro as an ethnic writer.

9. Gregory Mason, 'Inspiring Images: The Influence of Japanese Cinema on the Writings of Kazuo Ishiguro', *East–West Film Journal*, 3/2 (1989), 51. Most Western writers of Asian ancestry prefer this term to 'oriental', for now obvious reasons. Thus, 'Asian-Anglo' would be an appropriate designation for a writer like Ishiguro.

10. John Rothfork, 'Zen Comedy in Postcolonial Literature: Kazuo Ishiguro's *The Remains of the Day*', *Mosaic*, 29/1 (1996), 100, has not read the author's own remarks that his views stem directly from his *Western* not necessarily Asian perceptions. Rothfork also has several textual errors in his analysis: for instance, the narrator of Ishiguro's second novel is Masuji Ono, not Ichiro Ono, as Rothfork writes.

11. Susie O'Brien, 'Serving a New World Order: Postcolonial Politics in Kazuo Ishiguro's *The Remains of the Day*', *Modern Fiction Studies*, 42/4 (1996), 802.

12. Meera Tamaya, 'Ishiguro's *Remains of the Day*: The Empire Strikes Back', *Modern Language Studies*, 22/2 (1992), 54.

13. Malcolm Bradbury, *The Modern British Novel* (New York: Penguin, 1994), 415.

14. Ibid. 414.

15. Ibid. 422. See pp. 422–7 for the specific discussion of Ishiguro's novels.

16. Jonathan Wilson, 'The Literary Life: A Very English Story', *New Yorker*, 6 Mar. 1995, 100.

17. Bradbury, *The Modern British Novel*, 401, 425. Presumably 'Mrs Torture' is a thinly veiled Mrs Thatcher in Rushdie's fiction.

18. Quoted in Stephen Clingman, *The Novels of Nadine Gordimer: History from the Inside* (2nd edn., Amherst, Mass.: University of Massachusetts Press, 1992), 1.

19. All told, his novels have been translated into about twenty-seven different languages.

20. Ishiguro complains of writers like Pynchon who are 'a little over-intellectualized for me'.

CHAPTER 2.   READING THE NOVELS

1. Wayne Booth, *The Rhetoric of Fiction* (2nd edn., Chicago: University of Chicago Press, 1983), 155.

2. Ihab Hassan, *The Dismemberment of Orpheus: Toward a Postmodern Literature* (2nd edn., Madison: University of Wisconsin Press, 1982), 3, 13.

3. David B. Morris, 'About Suffering: Voice, Genre, and Moral Community', in Arthur Kleinman, Veena Das, and Margaret Lock (eds.), *Social Suffering* (Berkeley and Los Angeles: University of California Press, 1997), 31.

4. Norman Holland, 'Unity Identify Text Self', in Jane P. Tompkins (ed.), *Reader-Response Criticism* (Baltimore: Johns Hopkins University Press, 1980), 131–2. 'Aesthetic of Reception' is the international term derived from the German *rezeptionsathetik* (roughly, 'affective stylistics'), while 'reader-response' criticism or theory is the preferred American one.

5. See Booth, *The Rhetoric of Fiction*, for a clarification of these important terms: 'actual', 'implied', and 'ideal' categories of authors and readers. 'Actual' refers to a real-life person, 'implied' a persona as presented in the text; and 'ideal' a super-intelligent, all-knowing presence.

6. Wolfgang Iser, 'The Reading Process: A Phenomenological Approach', in Tompkins (ed.), *Reader-Response Criticism*, 50.

7. Ibid. 51.

8. Ibid. 55.

9. Reed Way Dasenbrock, 'Do We Write the Text We Read?', in David H. Richter (ed.), *Falling into Theory: Conflicting Views on Reading Literature* (New York: Bedford Books, 1994), 247.

10. These temporal orders are typical of the ones used by structural theorists of narrative, and each is further explained by Gérard

Genette, *Narrative Discourse*, trans. Jane E. Lewin (Ithaca, NY: Cornell University Press, 1989). The theoretical terms for these orders are, respectively: prolepsis, analepsis, and anachrony.

11. Gerald Prince, ('Introduction to the Study of the Narratee', in Tompkins (ed.), *Reader-Response Criticism* 7–25) defines a *narratee* as 'the person(s) the narrator directly addresses'. This 'person' is neither the real, virtual, or ideal reader, but rather an enigmatic presence who witnesses the narrator's innermost struggles. I have chosen not to use this term in such precise theoretical ways, because the addressee invoked by each of the narrators here can also be the actual reader of the text.

12. Georges Poulet ('Criticism and the Experience of Interiority', in Tompkins (ed.), *Reader-Response Criticism*, 47) offers one of the classical phenomenological perspectives of reader-response theory.

13. Hans Robert Jauss, *Toward an Aesthetic of Reception*, trans. Timothy Bahti, intro. Paul de Man (Minneapolis: University of Minnesota Press, 1982), 24.

14. Catherine Belsey, *Critical Practice* (London: Methuen, 1980), 132.

15. Shlomith Rimmon-Kenan, *Narrative Fiction: Contemporary Poetics* (London: Methuen, 1983), 94–5.

16. Francis Wyndham, in *New Yorker*, 23 Oct. 1995, 90.

17. Paul de Man, 'Introduction', in Jauss, *Toward an Aesthetic of Reception*, p. xii.

18. Jauss, *Toward an Aesthetic of Reception*, 24.

19. Mikhail Bahktin, 'Discourse in the Novel', in *The Dialogic Imagination*, ed. Michael Holquist, trans. Caryl Emerson and Michael Holquist (Austin, Tex.: University of Texas Press, 1981), 299.

20. Gregory Mason, 'Inspiring Images: The Influence of Japanese Cinema on the Writings of Kazuo Ishiguro', *East–West Film Journal*, 3/2 (1989), 39–52.

21. Allan Young ('Suffering and the Origins of Traumatic Memory', in Arthur Kleinman, Veena Das, and Margaret Lock (eds.), *Social Suffering* (Berkeley and Los Angeles: University of California Press, 1997), 245–60) discusses the way the two overlap, and he notes the first is based on universal biology and the second on social codes.

22. Lawrence Graver, in *New York Times Book Review*, 8 Oct. 1989, 3.

23. Kathryn Morton, in *New York Times Book Review*, 8 June 1986, 19.

CHAPTER 3.   NARRATIVE AND MEMORY: *A PALE VIEW OF HILLS*

1. Edith Wyschogrod, *Spirit in Ashes: Hegel, Heidegger, and Man-Made*

Mass Death (New Haven: Yale University Press, 1985), 2.

2. Many early reviews of *A Pale View of Hills* note the paradox of Etsuko's calm tone when recalling devastation. See Paul Bailey's review for *Times Literary Supplement*, 19 Feb. 1982, Edith Milton's for *New York Times Book Review*, 9 May 1982, and Penelope Lively's for *Encounter* (June–July 1982). Hermione Lee (in 'Quiet Desolation', *New Republic*, 22 Jan. 1990) identifies the narrative tension in the first three of Ishiguro's novels and observes that Ishiguro renders painful moments 'with heart-breaking quietness' (p. 39).

3. Georges Poulet, 'Criticism and the Experience of Interiority', in Jane P. Tompkins (ed.), *Reader-Response Criticism* (Baltimore: Johns Hopkins University Press, 1980), 45.

4. Gregory Mason, 'Inspiring Images: The Influence of Japanese Cinema on the Writings of Kazuo Ishiguro', *East–West Film Journal'*, 3/2 (1989), 47.

5. Paul de Man, 'Impersonality in the Criticism of Maurice Blanchot', *Blindness and Insight: Essays in the Rhetoric of Contemporary Criticism* (Minneapolis: University of Minnesota Press, 1983), 75.

6. I discussed this aspect of Etsuko's narrative in great detail in my essay 'The Shame of Memory: Blanchot's Self-Dispossession in Ishiguro's *A Pale View of Hills*, *Clio*, 24/2 (1995), 127–45, where I define Etsuko's narrative as a form of 'un-working', or of dispossession of anguish.

7. See Gérard Genette (*Narrative Discourse*, trans. Jane E. Lewin (Ithaca, NY: Cornell University Press, 1989)) for a discussion of temporal schemes in literature. In particular, the temporal orders of prolepsis (anticipation), analepsis (flashback), and anachrony (discordance) are useful to reading Ishiguro's novels. I also discuss these schemes in my essay, 'The Shame of Memory.'

8. Wallace Martin, *Recent Theories of Narrative* (Ithaca, NY: Cornell University Press, 1986), 65.

9. Poulet, 'Criticism and the Experience of Interiority', 41.

10. Frank Kermode, *The Sense of an Ending: Studies in the Theory of Fiction* (London: Oxford University Press, 1966), 138.

11. Jeffrey Berman ('Personality (Double-Split-Multiple)', in Jean-Claude Signeuret, *Dictionary of Literary Themes and Motifs* (New York: Greenwood Press, 1988), 963–70) considers these synonyms: shadow self, alter ego, second self, the anti-self, opposing self, and secret self.

12. Brian W. Shaffer (*Understanding Kazuo Ishiguro* (Durham, SC: University of South Carolina Press, 1998), 27–32) has an original, if far-reaching, theory about the way Ishiguro represents death in this novel. Shaffer refers to the ancient Greek myth of Styx and to Freudian psychology as two 'dynamics' of the novel. Ishiguro

himself has indicated that he personally does not subscribe to Freudian psychology (MJ 22), but it is not inconceivable, according to Shaffer's view, that his novels may be read with those paradigms.

13. Wolfgang Iser, 'The Reading Process: A Phenomenological Approach', in Tompkins (ed.), *Reader-Response Criticism*, 56.

14. Tzvetan Todorov, 'Reading as Construction', in Susan R. Suleiman and Inge Crosman (eds.), *The Reader in the Text* (Princeton: Princeton University Press, 1980), 80.

15. See Fumio Yoshioka ('Beyond the Division of East and West: Kazuo Ishiguro's *A Pale View of Hills*', *Studies in English Literature* (1988), 71–86) for a discussion of the way Ishiguro places the Second World War in the background of the story of individual lives.

16. Todorov, 'Reading as Construction', 75.

17. Hermione Lee ('Quiet Desolation', *New Republic*, 9 May 1982) correctly observes that Ishiguro's uses of – or lack of uses of – definite articles in his titles (*A Pale View of Hills*, not *A Pale View of THE Hills*) produce an evasive quality about the book's meaning, which cause them to be 'open to amendment and uncertainty' (p. 36). She also notes that 'the titles hover on the borders of allegory [which] give off a similarly puzzling and contingent air' (p. 36).

18. Jerrold Packard (*Sons of Heaven* (New York: Collier, 1989)), offers a readable account of some aspects of Japanese history relevant to this novel. In particular, he discusses the post-war period corresponding to Ishiguro's novel, and he explains some of the values splintering Japanese society at that time. Even though Ishiguro disavows historical accuracy in his fictional texts, I find that the author is quite accurate in his psychological portrayals of people such as Etsuko and Sachiko who were trying to flee towards a better life than the one offered by bomb-ruined Nagasaki in the late 1940s.

19. Walter Benjamin, 'The Storyteller', in *Illuminations* (New York: Schocken, 1969), 84.

20. Todorov, 'Reading as Construction', 75.

CHAPTER 4.   DEFLECTING TRUTH IN MEMORY: *AN ARTIST OF THE FLOATING WORLD*

1. Maurice Blanchot, 'Michel Foucault as I Imagine Him', *Foucault/Blanchot*, trans. Jeffrey Mehlman and Brian Massumi (New York: Zone, 1987), 64.

2. Karlheinz Stierle, 'The Reading of Fictional Texts', in Susan R.

Suleiman and Inge Crosman (eds.), *The Reader in the Text* (Princeton: Princeton University Press, 1980), 104.

3. Jane P. Tompkins (in 'The Reader in History: The Changing Shape of Literary Response', in Jane P. Tompkins (ed.), *Reader-Response Criticism* (Baltimore: Johns Hopkins University Press, 1980), 201–32) rightly notes that the similarity between formalism (New Criticism) and reader-response criticism (aesthetic of reception theory) is sometimes obscured by the issue of 'whether meaning is to be located in the text or in the reader' (p. 201). The distinction between 'private' and 'public' forms of discourse, as expressed by Ono in this novel, can be helpful for 'the specification of meaning', which is important for the subtle difference between how Ono perceives himself and how his reader–listener perceives him.

4. Peter Larmarque and Stein Haugom Olsen, *Truth, Fiction, and Literature: A Philosophical Perspective* (Oxford: Clarendon Press, 1994), 77.

5. See Jacques Derrida ('Difference', in *Speech and Phenomena and Other Essays on Husserl's Theory of Signs*, trans. David B. Allison (Evanston, Ill.: Northwestern University Press, 1973), 129–60) for a classic discussion of the 'trace' (pp. 142–3), an important aspect of deconstruction theory. I also have in mind Derrida's 'temporalizing' of the trace in Ono's case, but I have pursued this discussion through a view of reception aesthetics, which focuses on Ono's 'fictionalization' of his self-portrait.

6. Maurice Blanchot, *The Gaze of Orpheus*, trans. Lydia Davis (New York: Station Hill Press, 1981), 29.

7. Stierle, 'The Reading of Fictional Texts', 87.

8. Wolfgang Iser, 'Interaction between Text and Reader', in Susan R. Suleiman and Inge Crosman (eds.), *The Reader in the Text* (Princeton: Princeton University Press, 1980), 111.

9. Adam Zachary Newton ('Telling Others: Secrecy and Recognition in Dickens, Barnes, and Ishiguro', in *Narrative Ethics* (Cambridge, Mass.: Harvard University Press, 1997), 241–85) is among the first to raise ethical concerns confronting Ishiguro's characters.

10. In V&H Ishiguro invokes a book by the Japanese writer, Junichiro Tanazaki, *The Makioka Sisters* (1957; New York: Vintage International, 1995), which appears to be the inspiration for Noriko's *maia*, or marriage negotiations, in his second novel. There are astonishing similarities in the way both Tanazaki and Ishiguro write about this dated social ritual for young Japanese women.

11. Bruce King, 'The New Internationalism: Shiva Naipaul, Salman Rushdie, Buchi Emecheta, Timothy Mo and Kazuo Ishiguro', in James Acheson (ed.), *The British and Irish Novel since 1960* (New York: St Martin's Press, 1991), 207, 208.

12. George Steiner, *Language and Silence: Essays on Language, Literature and the Inhuman* (New York: Atheneum, 1982), 22.

13. Georges Poulet, 'Criticism and the Experience of Interiority', in Tompkins (ed.), *Reader-Response Criticism*, 45.

14. This provocative view about the teacher pertains to the reception aesthetics produced by Ishiguro's second novel; the passage comes from Ross Chambers, *Story and Situation: Narrative Seduction and the Power of Fiction* (Minneapolis: University of Minnesota Press, 1984), 50–1.

15. Larmarque and Olsen, *Truth, Fiction, and Literature*, 156.

16. Walter Benjamin, 'Theses on the Philosophy of History', in *Illuminations* (New York: Schocken, 1969), 255.

17. Maurice Blanchot, *The Writing of the Disaster*, trans. Ann Smock (Lincoln, Nebr.: University of Nebraska Press, 1986), 64.

CHAPTER 5.   DISCLOSURE AND 'UNCONCEALMENT': *THE REMAINS OF THE DAY*

1. Samuel Beckett, *Molloy*, in *Three Novels by Samuel Beckett* (New York: Grove Press, 1965), 34.

2. Nearly all short reviews for this novel praise its author's technique and themes. Among essays and journal articles, criticism can be divided under three general topics. The first, which includes work by Susie O'Brien and Meera Tamaya, examines post-colonial elements in Ishiguro's fiction; the second, by Adam Zachary Newton, Kathleen Wall, and Cynthia F. Wong, analyses technical aspects of Ishiguro's narrative; the third, by Gregory Mason and John Rothfork, deals with thematic concerns linked to Ishiguro's Japanese heritage. Nearly all the critics offer an interpretation of Ishiguro's uses of public and private realism in their character analysis.

3. Adam Zachary Newton, 'Telling Others: Secrecy and Recognition in Dickens, Barnes and Ishiguro', in *Narrative Ethics* (Cambridge, Mass.: Harvard University Press, 1997), 270.

4. Shlomith Rimmon-Kenan, *Narrative Fiction: Contemporary Poetics* (London: Methuen, 1983), 94–5.

5. Kathleen Wall, '*The Remains of the Day* and its Challenges to Theories of Unreliable Narration', *Journal of Narrative Technique*, 24/1 (1994), 23.

6. Ibid. 22–3.

7. Meera Tamaya, 'Ishiguro's *Remains of the Day*: The Empire Strikes Back', *Modern Language Studies*, 22/2 (1992), 45, 50.

8. Newton, 'Telling Others', 282.

9. Stanley E. Fish, 'Literature in the Reader: Affective Stylistics', in Jane P. Tompkins (ed.), *Reader-Response Criticism* (Baltimore: Johns Hopkins University Press, 1980), 70–100.

10. Susie O'Brien, 'Serving a New World Order: Postcolonial Politics in Kazuo Ishiguro's *The Remains of the Day*', *Modern Fiction Studies*, 42/4 (1996), 789.

11. Jonathan Culler, 'Literary Competence', in Tompkins (ed.), *Reader-Response Criticism*, 117.

12. David Gurewich, in *New Criterion*, 8/4 (1989), 78.

13. Perhaps unconsciously, Ishiguro has indeed created a 'post-colonial novel' without intending to do so in either direct or subtle fashion. Susie O'Brien characterizes the ironic distance of Stevens as being produced by 'Stevens's first person account, a voice which ironically comments on the pathology of colonial nostalgia without even completely disavowing it' ('Serving a New World Order', 801). She further notes that 'this enunciatory disjunction [proves] that Ishiguro's novel can most clearly be read as a comment on the postcolonial condition' (p. 801). However, I remain committed to a reading of the novel that examines the *personal* implications of such historical forces; Stevens can be no more and no less reliable than actual historians who attempt to locate *truth* in any large scheme, like post-colonial politics.

14. David Lodge, 'The Unreliable Narrator', in *The Art of Fiction* (New York: Viking, 1992), 155.

15. Wallace Martin, *Recent Theories of Narrative* (Ithaca, NY: Cornell University Press, 1986), 135.

16. I discuss Poulet's theory in my chapter on *A Pale View of Hills*. Poulet's notion of selves splitting in the reading and writing processes has resonance for Etsuko, Ono, and Stevens. Unlike clinical schizophrenia, this concept is useful in narrative theory as a way of determining the degree of control or mastery exerted by the narrator. I have applied this option along the 'extradiegetic' and 'homodiegetic' levels of narration in Stevens's story in order to expand Ishiguro's narrative devices; all of the narrators in these novels undergo a similar process of 'splitting' into two distinct voices or personas – one reads and the other interprets the way the past shaped him or her.

17. Ibid. 45.

18. Maurice Blanchot, *The Gaze of Orpheus*, trans. Lydia Davis (New York: Station Hill Press, 1981), 138.

19. Ishiguro identifies one of his concerns as 'how people use the language of self-deception and self-protection' in their lives (GM 337).

CHAPTER 6. SEIZING COMPREHENSION: *THE UNCONSOLED*

1. George Steiner, *Real Presences* (Chicago: University of Chicago Press, 1989), 139.
2. Zygmunt Bauman, *Mortality, Immortality and Other Life Strategies* (Stanford, Calif.: Stanford University Press, 1992), 66–7.
3. Vince Passaro, 'New Flash from an Old Isle', *Harper's Magazine* (Oct. 1995), 75.
4. Maurice Blanchot, 'Knowledge of the Unknown', in *The Infinite Conversation*, trans. Susan Hanson (Minneapolis: University of Minnesota Press, 1993), 50. This relatively complex theory of how postmodern subjects can 'know' themselves or their circumstances has a long philosophical tradition, which is somewhat beyond the aims of this book on Ishiguro. I introduce this 'negative' theory at this stage, because Ishiguro's fiction underscores an epistemological crisis affecting modern and postmodern peoples.
5. Shlomith Rimmon-Kenan, *Narrative Fiction: Contemporary Poetics* (London: Methuen, 1983), 79.
6. Karlheinz Stierle, 'The Reading of Fictional Texts', in Susan R. Suleiman and Inge Crosman (eds.), *The Reader in the Text* (Princeton: Princeton University Press, 1980), 83.
7. Charlotte Innes, 'Fiction without Frontiers', *Los Angeles Times*, 5 Nov. 1995, 11.
8. Charlotte Innes, 'Dr Faustus Faces the Music', *Nation*, 6 Nov. 1995, 546.
9. James Wood, 'Ishiguro's Machine for Self-Humiliation', *Manchester Guardian Weekly*, 21 May 1995, 37.
10. Sybil Steinberg, 'Kazuo Ishiguro: "A Book About Our World"', *Publisher's Weekly*, 18 Sept. 1995, 105.
11. Some other early critical reviews of the novel are worth noting. Alan Wall ('A Long Look at Nothing Much', *Spectator*, 13 May 1995) has as his main complaint the novel's length, and he is so thoroughly daunted by this obvious contrast to Ishiguro's early work that he then tries to read what he hopes are allusions to Franz Kafka and Samuel Beckett in this novel. Anita Brookner's intelligent assessment of the novel ('A Superb Achievement', *Spectator*, 24 June 1995) appears to be commissioned by the editors of that publication in an effort to address Wall's more hopeless efforts of the previous month. Somewhat more pedestrian reviews of the non-committed sort appear by Paul Gray ('Bad Dream', *Time Magazine*, 2 Oct. 1995) and Guy Lawson ('Musical and Narrative Chaos', *Maclean's*, 22 May 1995). Both express nostalgia for *The Remains of the Day* and imply that Ishiguro should write more novels

of the early kind. Ned Rorem ('Fiction in Review', *Yale Review*, 84/2 (1996)) offers one of the most puzzling and lengthiest complaints about the novel. Admitting to having no knowledge of Ishiguro's work and its substance, he fails to grasp most of the author's literary innovations.

12. The arrival/return to an unfamiliar, but strangely familiar city calls to mind work produced by the French writer Alain Robbe-Grillet. In particular, *Les Gommes* (trans. *The Erasers* (New York: Grove Press, 1964)), has a very similar theme of disoriented wandering; also, Robbe-Grillet's impact on *nouveau roman*, or the 'new novel', in the 1950s seems to foreshadow much of the spirit and innovation of fiction that characterizes Ishiguro's fourth novel.

13. On 15 Oct. 1995, Ishiguro 'explained' the novel to a Denver, Colorado (USA), audience at his book-signing.

14. Herbert Blau, 'Universals of Performance', *The Eye of Prey: Subversions of the Postmodern* (Bloomington, Ind.: Indiana University Press, 1987), 163.

15. Steiner, *Real Presences*, 124.

16. Blanchot, 'Knowledge of the Unknown', 50–1.

·

Select Bibliography

WORKS BY KAZUO ISHIGURO

Novels

A Pale View of Hills (London: Faber & Faber; New York: G.P. Putnam's Sons, 1982; paperback edn., New York: Vintage International, 1990).

An Artist of the Floating World (London: Faber & Faber; New York: G. P. Putnam's Sons, 1986; paperback edn., New York: Vintage International, 1989).

The Remains of the Day (London: Faber & Faber; New York: Knopf, 1989; paperback edn., New York: Vintage International, 1993).

The Unconsoled (London: Faber & Faber; New York: Knopf, 1995; paperback edn., New York: Vintage International, 1996).

When We Were Orphans (London: Faber & Faber, 2000).

Short Works

'A Family Supper', *Esquire* (March 1990), 207–11.

'Getting Poisoned', *Introduction 7: Stories by New Writers* (London: Faber & Faber, 1981), 38–51.

'A Strange and Sometimes Sadness', *Introduction 7: Stories by New Writers* (London: Faber & Faber, 1981), 13–27.

'Summer after the War', *Granta*, 7 (1983), 120–37.

'Waiting for J', *Introduction 7: Stories by New Writers* (London: Faber & Faber, 1981), 28–37.

'The Gourmet', *Granta*, 43 (1993), 89–127.

INTERVIEWS WITH KAZUO ISHIGURO

Jaggi, Maya, 'Kazuo Ishiguro Talks to Maya Jaggi', *Wasafiri*, 22 (1995), 20–4.

Krider, Dylan Otto, 'Rooted in a Small Space: An Interview with Kazuo Ishiguro', *Kenyon Review*, 20/2 (1998), 146–54.

Mason, Gregory, 'An Interview with Kazuo Ishiguro', *Contemporary Literature*, 30/3 (1989), 335–47.

Oe, Kenzaburo, and Ishiguro, Kazuo, 'The Novelist in Today's World: A Conversation', *Boundary 2*, 18/3 (1991), 109–22.

Vorda, Alan, and Herzinger, Kim, 'An Interview with Kazuo Ishiguro', *Mississippi Review*, 20 (1991), 131–54. Also appears in Allan Vorda (ed.), *Face to Face: Interviews with Contemporary Novelists* (Houston: Rice University Press, 1993), 1–35.

SHORT REVIEWS OF NOVELS BY KAZUO ISHIGURO

On *A Pale View of Hills*

Bailey, Paul, *Times Literary Supplement*, 19 Feb. 1982, 179.

Lee, Hermione, *New Republic*, 22 Jan. 1990, 36–9.

Lively, Penelope, *Encounter* (June–July 1982), 86–91.

Milton, Edith, *New York Times Book Review*, 9 May 1982, 12–13.

On *An Artist of the Floating World*

Hunt, Nigel, *Brick: A Journal of Reviews* (Fall 1987), 36–8.

Morton, Kathryn, *New York Times Book Review*, 8 June 1986, 19.

Parrinder, Patrick, *London Review of Books*, 6 Feb. 1986, 16–17.

On *The Remains of the Day*

Atkinson, Rob, *Yale Law Journal*, 105/1 (1995), 177.

Bloom, Alice, *Hudson Review*, 43 (1990), 156–64.

Graver, Lawrence, *New York Times Book Review*, 8 Oct. 1989, 3, 33.

Gurewich, David, *New Criterion*, 8/4 (1989), 77–80.

Hassan, Ihab, *World and I*, 5/2 (Feb. 1990), 368–74.

Iyer, Pico, *Partisan Review*, 58 (1991), 585–90.

Kamine, Mark, *New Leader* (Nov. 1989), 21–2.

King, Francis, *Spectator* (1989), 31–2.

Lee, Sasanne Wah, *Nation*, 18 Dec. 1989, 761–3.

Slay, J., *Explicator*, 55/3 (1997), 180.

Strawson, Galen, *Times Literary Supplement*, 19 May 1989, 535.

Swift, Graham, *Bomb*, 29 (1989), 22–3.

On *The Unconsoled*

Blythe, Will, *New Yorker*, 28/41 (1995), 64.

Brookner, Anita, *Spectator*, 24 June 1995, 40–1.

Chaudhuri, Amit, *London Review of Books*, 8 June 1995, 30.

Cusk, Rachel, *The Times*, 11 May 1995, 38.

Gray, Paul, *Time Magazine*, 2 Oct. 1995, 81–2.

Innes, Charlotte, *Los Angeles Times*, 5 Nov. 1995, 11.

——— *Nation*, 6 Nov. 1995, 546–8.

Iyer, Pico, *Times Literary Supplement*, 28 Apr. 1995, 22.

Kauffman, Stanley, *New Republic*, 6 Nov. 1995, 42.

Kaveney, Roz, *New Statesman and Society*, 12 May 1995, 39.

Lawson, Guy, *Maclean's*, 22 May 1995.

Menand, Louis, *New York Times Book Review*, 15 Oct. 1995, 7.

Passaro, Vince, *Harper's Magazine* (Oct. 1995), 71–5.

Rorem, Ned, *Yale Review*, 84/2 (1996), 154.

Rorty, Richard, *Village Voice Literary Supplement* (Oct. 1995), 13.

Rubin, Merle, *Christian Science Monitor*, 4 Oct. 1995, 14.

Shone, Tom, *Harper's Bazaar*, 1 Oct. 1995, 132.

Steinberg, Sybil, *Publisher's Weekly*, 18 Sept. 1995, 105–6.

Sweet, Nick, *Contemporary Review*, 267 (1995), 223–4.

Wall, Alan, *Spectator*, 13 May 1995, 45.

Wood, James, *Manchester Guardian Weekly*, 21 May 1995, 37.

Wyndham, Francis, *New Yorker*, 23 Oct. 1995, 90.

CRITICAL ESSAYS, ARTICLES, AND BOOKS

Davis, Rocio, 'Imaginary Homelands Revisited in the Novels of Kazuo Ishiguro', *Miscelanea*, 15 (1994), 139–54.

Griffiths, M., 'Great English Houses/New Homes in England? Memory and Identity in Kazuo Ishiguro's *The Remains of the Day* and V. S. Naipaul's *The Enigma of Arrival*', *SPAN*, 36 (1993), 488–503.

Habib, C., 'Nagasaki and More: On the English Novels of Kazuo Ishiguro', *Espirit*, 2 (1991), 114–20.

Janik, Del Ivan, 'No End of History: Evidence from the Contemporary English Novel', *Twentieth-Century Literature* (Summer 1995), 1–27.

King, Bruce, 'The New Internationalism: Shiva Naipaul, Salman Rushdie, Buchi Emecheta, Timothy Mo and Kazuo Ishiguro', in James Acheson (ed.), *The British and Irish Novel since 1960* (New York: St Martin's Press, 1991), 192–211.

Lodge, David, 'The Unreliable Narrator', in *The Art of Fiction* (New York: Viking, 1992), 154–7.

Mallett, Peter J., 'The Revelation of Character in Kazuo Ishiguro's *The Remains of the Day* and *An Artist of the Floating World*', *Shoin Literary Review*, 29 (1996), 1–20.

Mason, Gregory, 'Inspiring Images: The Influence of Japanese Cinema on the Writings of Kazuo Ishiguro', *East–West Film Journal*, 3/2 (1989), 39–52.

Newton, Adam Zachary, 'Telling Others: Secrecy and Recognition in Dickens, Barnes, and Ishiguro', in *Narrative Ethics* (Cambridge, Mass.: Harvard University Press, 1997), 241–85. 4 BP New

O'Brien, Susie, 'Serving a New World Order: Postcolonial Politics in Kazuo Ishiguro's *The Remains of the Day*, *Modern Fiction Studies*, 42/4 (1996), 787–806. PS Ab bay8

Patey, Caroline, 'When Ishiguro Visits the West Country: An Essay on *The Remains of the Day*', *Acme*, 44/2 (1991), 135–55. Slock PR Z Bay 2

Rothfork, John, 'Zen Comedy in Postcolonial Literature: Kazuo Ishiguro's *The Remains of the Day*', *Mosaic*, 29/1 (1996), 79–102. PS AB

Rushdie, Salman, '"Commonwealth Literature" Does Not Exist' and 'Kazuo Ishiguro', in *Imaginary Homelands: Essays and Criticism, 1981–1991* (London: Viking, 1991), 61–70 and 244–6. Red 4 UB 7 Rus

Shaffer, Brian W., *Understanding Kazuo Ishiguro* (Durham, SC: University of South Carolina Press, 1998).

Tamaya, Meera, 'Ishiguro's *Remains of the Day*: The Empire Strikes Back', *Modern Language Studies*, 22/2 (1992), 45–56.

Wain, Peter, 'The Historical–Political Aspect of the Novels of Kazuo Ishiguro', *Language and Culture*, 23 (1992), 177–205.

Wall, Kathleen, '*The Remains of the Day* and its Challenges to Theories of Unreliable Narration', *Journal of Narrative Technique*, 24/1 (1994), 18–42. PS Ab

Watson, George, 'The Silence of the Servants', *Sewanne Review*, 103/3 (1995), 480–6.

Wilson, Jonathan, 'The Literary Life: A Very English Story', *New Yorker*, 6 Mar. 1995, 96–106.

Wong, Cynthia F., 'The Shame of Memory: Blanchot's Self-Dispossession in Ishiguro's *A Pale View of Hills*', *Clio*, 24/2 (1995), 127–45.

Yoshioka, Fumio, 'Beyond the Division of East and West: Kazuo Ishiguro's *A Pale View of Hills*', *Studies in English Literature* (1998), 71–86.

OTHER WORKS MENTIONED IN THE TEXT

Bauman, Zygmunt, 'Mortality, Immortality and Other Life Strategies (Stanford, Calif.: Stanford University Press, 1992).

Belsey, Catherine, *Critical Practice* (London: Methuen, 1980).

Bakhtin, Mikhail, 'Discourse in the Novel', in *The Dialogic Imagination*, ed. Michael Holquist, trans. Caryl Emerson and Michael Holquist (Austin, Tex.: University of Texas Press, 1981), 259–422.

Benjamin, Walter, 'The Storyteller' and 'Theses on the Philosophy of History', in *Illuminations* (New York: Schocken, 1969), 83–109, 253–64.

Berman, Jeffrey, 'Personality (Double–Split–Multiple)', in Jean-Claude Signeuret, *Dictionary of Literary Themes and Motifs* (New York:

Greenwood Press, 1988), 963–70.

Blanchot, Maurice, 'Michel Foucault as I Imagine Him', in *Foucault/ Blanchot*, trans. Jeffrey Mehlman and Brian Massumi (New York: Zone, 1987).

—— *The Gaze of Orpheus*, trans. Lydia Davis (New York: Station Hill Press, 1981).

—— 'Knowledge of the Unknown', in *The Infinite Conversation*, trans. Susan Hanson (Minneapolis: University of Minnesota Press, 1993).

—— *The Writing of the Disaster*, trans. Ann Smock (Lincoln, Nebr.: University of Nebraska Press, 1986).

Blau, Herbert, *The Eye of Prey: Subversions of the Postmodern* (Bloomington, Ind.: Indiana University Press, 1987).

Booth, Wayne, *The Rhetoric of Fiction* (2nd edn., Chicago: University of Chicago Press, 1983).

Bradbury, Malcolm, *The Modern British Novel* (New York: Penguin, 1994).

Chambers, Ross, *Story and Situation: Narrative Seduction and the Power of Fiction* (Minneapolis: University of Minnesota Press, 1984).

Clingman, Stephen, *The Novels of Nadine Gordimer: History from the Inside* (2nd edn., Amherst, Mass.: University of Massachusetts Press, 1992).

Culler, Jonathan, 'Literary Competence', in Jane P. Tompkins (ed.), *Criticism* (Baltimore: Johns Hopkins University Press, 1980), 101–17.

Dasenbrock, Reed Way, 'Do We Write the Text We Read?' in David A. Richter (ed.), *Falling into Theory: Conflicting Views on Reading Literature* (New York: Bedford Books, 1994), 238–48.

de Man, Paul, 'Impersonality in the Criticism of Maurice Blanchot', in *Blindness and Insight: Essays in the Rhetoric of Contemporary Criticism* (Minneapolis: University of Minnesota Press, 1983), 60–78.

Derrida, Jacques, 'Differance', in *Speech and Phenomenon and Other Essays on Husserl's Theory of Signs*, trans. David B. Alleson (Evanston, Ill.: Northwestern University Press, 1973), 129–60.

Fish, Stanley, E., 'Literature in the Reader: Affective Stylistics', in Jane P. Tompkins (ed.), *Reader-Response Criticism* (Baltimore: Johns Hopkins University Press, 1980), 70–100.

Genette, Gérard, *Narrative Discourse*, trans. Jane E. Lewin (Ithaca, NY: Cornell University Press, 1989).

Hassan, Ihab, *The Dismemberment of Orpheus: Toward a Postmodern Literature* (2nd edn., Madison: University of Wisconsin Press, 1982).

Holland, Norman, 'Unity Identity Text Self', in Jane P. Tompkins (ed.), *Reader-Response Criticism* (Baltimore: Johns Hopkins University Press, 1980), 118–33.

Iser, Wolfgang, 'Interaction between Text and Reader', in Susan R. Suleiman and Inge Crosman (eds.), *The Reader in the Text* (Princeton: Princeton University Press, 1980), 106–19.

—— 'The Reading Process: A Phenomenological Approach', in Jane P.

Tompkins (ed.), *Reader-Response Criticism* (Baltimore: Johns Hopkins University Press, 1980), 50–69.

Jauss, Hans Robert, *Toward an Aesthetic of Reception*, trans. Timothy Bahti, intro. Paul de Man (Minneapolis: University of Minnesota Press, 1982).

Kermode, Frank, *The Sense of an Ending: Studies in the Theory of Fiction* (London: Oxford University Press, 1966).

Larmarque, Peter, and Olsen, Stein Haugom, *Truth, Fiction, and Literature: A Philosophical Perspective* (Oxford: Clarendon Press, 1994).

Lukács, Georg, *The Theory of the Novel*, trans. Anna Bostock (Cambridge, Mass.: MIT Press, 1971).

Martin, Wallace, *Recent Theories of Narrative* (Ithaca, NY: Cornell University Press, 1986).

Morris, David B., 'About Suffering: Voice, Genre and Moral Community', in Arthur Kleinman, Veena Das, and Margaret Lock (eds.), *Social Suffering* (Berkeley and Los Angeles: University of California Press, 1997), 25–45.

Packard, Jerrold, *Sons of Heaven* (New York: Collier, 1989).

Poulet, Georges, 'Criticism and the Experience of Interiority', in Jane P. Tompkins (ed.), *Reader-Response Criticism* (Baltimore: Johns Hopkins University Press, 1980), 41–9.

Prince, Gerald, 'Introduction to the Study of the Narratee', in Jane P. Tompkins (ed.), *Reader-Response Criticism* (Baltimore: Johns Hopkins University Press, 1980), 7–25.

Rimmon-Kenan, Shlomith, *Narrative Fiction: Contemporary Poetics* (London: Methuen, 1983).

Said, Edward W., *Orientalism* (New York: Vintage Books, 1979).

Stierle, Karlheinz, 'The Reading of Fictional Texts', in Susan R. Suleiman and Inge Crosman (eds.), *The Reader in the Text* (Princeton: Princeton University Press, 1980), 83–105.

Steiner, George, *Language and Silence: Essays on Language, Literature and the Inhuman* (New York: Atheneum, 1982).

—— *Real Presences* (Chicago: University of Chicago Press, 1989).

Tompkins, Jane P., 'The Reader in History: The Changing Shape of Literary Response', in Jane P. Tompkins (ed.), *Reader-Response Criticism* (Baltimore: Johns Hopkins University Press, 1980), 50–69.

Todorov, Tzvetan, 'Reading as Construction', in Susan R. Suleiman and Inge Crosman (eds.), *The Reader in the Text* (Princeton: Princeton University Press, 1980), 67–82.

Wyschogrod, Edith, *Spirit in Ashes: Hegel, Heidegger, and Man-Made Mass Death* (New Haven: Yale University Press, 1985).

Young, Allan, 'Suffering and the Origins of Traumatic Memory', in Arthur Kleinman, Veena Das, and Margaret Lock (eds.), *Social Suffering* (Berkeley and Los Angeles: University of California Press, 1997), 245–60.

Index